Becoming a Higher Level Teaching Assistant: Primary Special Educational Needs

The Professional Teaching Assistant

Becoming a Higher Level Teaching Assistant: Primary Special Educational Needs

Mary Doveston
and Steve
Cullingford-
Agnew

m

Learning Matters

Every effort has been made to trace copyright holders and to obtain their permission for the use of copyright material. The author and publisher will gladly receive any information enabling them to rectify any error or omission in subsequent editions.

First published in 2006 by Learning Matters Ltd.

British Library Cataloguing in Publication Data
A CIP record for this book is available from the British Library.

ISBN 13: 978 1 84445 052 7
ISBN 10: 1 84445 052 X

Project Management by Deer Park Productions
Cover design by Code 5 Design Associates Ltd
Typeset by Pantek Arts Ltd, Maidstone, Kent
Printed and bound in Great Britain by Bell & Bain Ltd, Glasgow

Learning Matters Ltd
33 Southernhay East
EXETER EX1 1NX
Tel: 01392 215560
info@learningmatters.co.uk
www.learningmatters.co.uk

Contents

The authors

Mary Doveston is a Senior Lecturer in Special Education at the University of Northampton. She has taught in all phases of education and has recently held posts as a special needs co-ordinator in a junior school and as a specialist teacher for special educational needs in Northamptonshire LEA. She is currently a trainer and assessor for HLTA at the University of Northampton.

Steve Cullingford-Agnew is a Senior Lecturer in Education working for the Centre for Special Education and Research Team at the University of Northampton. He has previously held posts as a head teacher at special schools in Northamptonshire and has worked as a LEA SEN inspector. He is currently a trainer and assessor for HLTA at the University of Northampton.

Acknowledgements

The authors are indebted to colleagues in the CeSNER team within the School of Education at the University of Northampton for their ideas, encouragement, help and advice. We are also grateful to the colleagues and pupils at Kingsley Special School, NIAS and the many teaching assistants with whom we have worked and who have participated on courses provided through the School of Education.

Dedication

This book is dedicated to all the teaching assistants with whom we have worked in schools and on CPD courses, in gratitude for their enthusiasm, commitment, creativity and sensitivity in their work in supporting all pupils, especially those with special educational needs.

Introduction

HOW TO USE THIS BOOK

This book, along with the others in the *Professional Teaching Assistant* series, has been designed not only to assist you in achieving HLTA status, but also to encourage you to reflect upon and learn about the requirements of working in today's classrooms. This book is written in recognition of the fact that the important role played by teaching assistants (TAs) in our schools and colleges is finally being acknowledged, and that increasing numbers of TAs are seeking further training, qualifications and status within their schools.

This book is designed to inform the thinking and practice of professional TAs who are teaching and supporting pupils with special educational needs (SEN) in mainstream and special schools. As it is likely, however, that all TAs will work with pupils with special needs at some time in their career, it is hoped that this book will be of interest to a wider readership.

This book begins with the premise that its readers have made a commitment to achieving the highest standards in providing classroom support for all pupils. It sets out not only to assist the reader in gaining the standards for HLTA, but also provides opportunities for reflection upon how pupils learn and how they may best be supported in that process.

It is anticipated that those who read this book are likely to have embarked upon a pathway, which they hope will lead them to gaining HLTA status. With this in mind the book has been written to a set format which aims to assist the reader in gaining some understanding of issues, encourages them to consider these in respect of specific examples and to undertake a series of tasks to develop their own thinking and subject knowledge.

Each chapter has a brief introduction, which is followed by an outline of the HLTA Standards to be considered within the chapter. Inevitably, some of the standards will be addressed in more than one chapter, while others are more tightly focused and may only be considered at a specific point in the book. Early in each chapter you will find a box which outlines what you should have learned once you have read the chapter and completed the tasks within it.

Chapter 2 outlines the legislation which both informs and reflects current principles and practice in meeting the needs of pupils with special educational needs. The three principles of inclusion set out in the National Curriculum Inclusion Statement (1999) are clearly interwoven into the chapters that follow:

- setting suitable learning challenges
- responding to pupils' diverse learning needs
- overcoming potential barriers to learning and assessment for individuals and groups of pupils.

Chapter 3 focuses on individual education plans, which define appropriate targets, teaching strategies and support to enable a pupil with SEN to learn most effectively. Chapters 4 and 7 discuss how professional TAs can work with teachers to set appropriate learning objectives and assess the progress of all pupils.

Chapters 5, 6 and 7 explore how potential barriers to learning and assessment may be overcome through multi-sensory teaching, a variety of assessment opportunities and different access strategies.

Chapter 8 examines the role of the TA working in partnership with parents and other professionals and is particularly pertinent with the recent publication of the Children Act (2004) and Removing Barriers to Achievement (2004).

The book concludes with Chapter 9, which highlights the important role that TAs can play in facilitating pupils to contribute to their learning and in ensuring that their views are heard and valued.

The case studies have all been drawn from the school experiences of colleagues and students with whom we have worked over the years. They are presented as a means of illustrating principles discussed in the chapter. You may consider these in respect of your own experiences and should always try to reflect upon them in a way that enables you to think about how you would deal with similar situations in your own school.

The practical tasks provided are designed to encourage you to gather evidence of your own, or your school's response to a range of situations related to the HLTA Standards. In some instances you may choose to use the evidence gathered from undertaking these tasks as a contribution towards the assessment process. For some of the tasks you will need the co-operation of colleagues or others within your school. It is hoped that by participating in these tasks you may be enabled to engage in a professional dialogue which informs your own thinking and possibly that of others.

At the end of each chapter you will find a summary of key points which indicate some of the most important principles discussed and which you may wish to consider in respect of your own practice and that of others within your school.

This book draws upon research and refers to a number of other key texts but does so without wishing to overburden the reader with the task of needing to hunt for additional information unless they should choose so to do. The references are listed at the end of each chapter and provide an indication of further reading which you may wish to pursue as you continue your path towards attaining HLTA status.

1. Meeting the Standards for the Higher Level Teaching Assistant

This book has been written with the aim of helping you to prepare for the new status of the Higher Level Teaching Assistant (HLTA) and focuses on the needs of pupils with special educational needs. It may be that you wish to cite special educational needs as a specialist area in your HLTA assessment or perhaps you aim to improve your competence and confidence in this area of the curriculum. It will also be valuable to those who just want to improve their practice in supporting special educational needs (SEN) or who are enrolled on foundation courses.

In the publication *Time for Standards*, the government set out its plans for the reform of the school workforce. This reform recognised that support staff can, and do, make an increasingly critical contribution to all aspects of the successful operation of schools. At the same time there was an important acknowledgement that with training and support many TAs can operate at a higher level than may have been recognised in the past.

The HLTA standards were published in September 2003 (TTA 2004a) and revised in April 2005. They identify those skills and the understanding you will need to demonstrate in order to be awarded the status of HLTA. Many TAs when they first look at these standards suggest that they already meet many, if not all, of them. You will find when we look at the standards in detail that this is often the case but that some standards may be more problematic to demonstrate than others. This may because of the specific situation in which you have been working, or related to a lack of training in respect of certain elements of the standards. However the key point to understand is that the status of HLTA is awarded by the Training and Development Agency for Schools (TDA, formerly the Teacher Training Agency (TTA)) via a number of approved training providers and that you will need to provide evidence to them that you can meet all of the standards as detailed. The main focus of this chapter is to help you to become familiar with the standards and to help you prepare for this assessment. Not every standard is applicable to Special Educational Needs but many are, and reference is made to these throughout the book.

There are a number of underlying principles which inform the assessment of HLTA, and these can be identified under the following headings:

Assessment of HLTA status:

- School support for the candidate.
- Proficiency in literacy and numeracy (see Standard 2.6).
- Assessment must be manageable, rigorous and fit for purpose.
- Assessment must take no more time than is necessary to demonstrate competence.
- Assessment should be based on work that occurs during the normal course of duties.
- It is the responsibility of the candidate to record evidence in support of the assessment.

The first of these principles is important for anyone contemplating going forward for assessment. The support of the school is essential if you are to be able to gather all of the evidence which you require in order to demonstrate that you meet the required standards. Your head teacher will have to agree to your application to go on a HLTA route. It is also helpful to discuss this procedure with your immediate working colleagues who you will be asking to support you at various stages of the process. It is equally essential that you have a literacy or numeracy qualification at NVQ level 2 or its equivalent, as you will not be able to proceed successfully without this crucial evidence. Details of what constitutes these levels are available from the TDA website **www.tda.gov.uk**. The aim of the HLTA programme is that the assessment process should be linked to your normal workload, in other words, you should be in a position to use evidence from your daily working practice in order to support the assessment process. This aim, whilst laudable, has not, in most cases, been realised and the majority of candidates have undertaken a large amount of additional work in order to ensure that they gain sufficient evidence to satisfy the assessors.

There are three routes to achieving HLTA status. These are:

1. Assessment only route, this is a three-day route spread over a term and is for more experienced TAs who feel that they already meet the standards.
2. Training route. This provides face to face training. The length and nature of this training is based upon a needs analysis. Candidates will opt into the training sessions they require. This route is for TAs who need training in certain standards before they apply for HLTA status.
3. Specialist HLTA routes for candidates working within just one curriculum area within a secondary school.

An early priority must be for you to decide which is the best route for you. This depends on your current level of expertise and training and your personal confidence in relation to the HLTA Standards. This is where having the support of colleagues in school may be particularly helpful in providing you with an opportunity to discuss how both you and they feel about your current experience and expertise. If you have limited experience of working in schools as a TA and have undertaken very limited training you need to explore how you can extend your knowledge and experience and then apply to go on a HLTA route in the future. If you feel that you need further training in order to meet the standards, for example in the areas of Special Educational Needs (SEN) or Information and Communications Technology (ICT), then the full training route is likely to be the most appropriate for you. As mentioned above, this is based on a needs analysis and you will select the relevant training sessions. This training will be provided through face to face training and computer-based e-learning.

If you feel that you have considerable knowledge, experience and skills related to the HLTA Standards you should apply to go on the assessment only route. However, we would advise that before making this decision, you examine the HLTA Standards carefully in order to ensure that you are familiar with these, and will be able to provide clear evidence of your ability to meet them in assessment. The task at the end of this chapter is designed to enable you to do this.

The specialist HLTA route is aimed at TAs working in secondary schools, particularly where they are supporting within a single curriculum area. At the time of writing, this route is in the early stages of development.

Another possible route to HLTA is for those students who are taking a foundation degree or similar degree course. The increase in opportunities to undertake foundation degrees has, in many instances, been welcomed by TAs as enabling them to further their own professional knowledge and skills. You will still need to apply for a place on the HLTA via your local Local Education Authority (LEA) and undertake the assessment only route.

There are a number of stages for you to go through and some TAs reading this book will already be on a HLTA programme, while others are considering applying. The six stages for the three day assessment route are:

- Candidate information
- Two day briefing
- Assessment tasks
- One day briefing and review
- School visit
- Decision communicated

PRACTICAL TASK

Consider the position of the following TAs who are considering being assessed for the HLTA. Which of the three assessment routes would you recommend to them and why?

Susan is a TA currently working within the Foundation stage. She is currently working towards a foundation degree for TAs and hopes to achieve Qualified Teacher Status. There are two Reception classes in the Foundation stage in her school and Susan plans, and delivers sessions on numeracy and creative developments. Susan works closely with the Reception teacher. Susan wants to achieve HLTA status as a way of getting onto an employment based route into teaching.

John is a TA who has worked in the school for one year and has an excellent awareness of autism spectrum disorders. He works with a Year 5 pupil who has a diagnosis of autistic spectrum disorder and now would like to expand his opportunities to work across the school with other pupils.

Angela has undertaken a number of courses for TAs at her local university and worked as a specialist TA for six years. She works with individual pupils, groups and a whole class for dance. She has experience of teaching dance to children and adults at her local community centre.

It is possible to suggest that in the examples provided, John should do the full training route, Angela an assessment course and Susan needs to opt for the assessment only route as she is undertaking a foundation degree. However, much will depend upon the individual circumstances of the interested TAs as well as factors such as the support of the school in providing opportunities for gaining experience and the confidence with which they each approach the task. These are important factors which you need to consider in committing yourself to this process. Which ever route is most relevant to you, you will have to undertake the same assessment procedures as all the candidates on the other routes.

Motivation

It is essential that all TAs who approach the route towards gaining HLTA status consider those factors which motivate them. There are many reasons why you may wish to undertake this pathway.

Most experienced TAs like Susan and Angela would identify that their jobs have changed compared with when they started. Susan is completing a foundation degree in Teaching and Learning and is using the HLTA status as a stepping stone to her ultimate professional goal of becoming a teacher. She has already identified an ambitious pathway which will ultimately lead her to further qualifications in order to join the teaching profession. Angela and John have not, at present identified the HLTA as leading to a career move. Indeed, they both see the enhanced status of HLTA as their ultimate work related goal. This, for many professional colleagues will be sufficient in itself as a motivating factor in undertaking the HLTA pathway. The HLTA is not intended as a stepping stone towards gaining a teaching qualification, though some colleagues may find that it is a useful starting point which can be used towards attaining a place on further training courses which may lead to this goal. Whatever your motivation for embarking on the HLTA, you are beginning a process which will lead to a recognition of your professionalism and will be recognised across educational institutions as an acknowledgement of your skills, knowledge and understanding.

Understanding the HLTA Standards

The HLTA Standards have been designed as a means of assessing your skills, knowledge and understanding as a professional and are divided into 3 sections, these being:

1. Professional Values and Practice – 1.1 to 1.6
2. Knowledge and Understanding – 2.1 to 2.9
3. Teaching and Learning Activities, these are further subdivided into:
   a) Planning and Expectations – 3.1.1 to 3.1.4
   b) Monitoring and Assessment – 3.2.1 to 3.2.4
   c) Teaching and Learning Activities – 3.3.1 to 3.3.8

You will be aware of these standards if you have begun the application process. It is likely that on viewing these you may feel that some are fairly straightforward whilst others are more complex. It is probable that some standards will require some clarification. For example Standard 2.7 is *They are aware of the statutory frameworks relevant to their role.*

With this standard there is a need to specify the extent of the knowledge and understanding expected of TAs working at a HLTA level. It is important to specify what is expected of their role and how this expectation will change from, for example, a TA working in a Year 6 class to one working in a nursery school. It is quite probable that you may be more familiar with some of the statutory requirements which relate directly to your current role. For example, if you are working as a TA supporting pupils with special educational needs, you may well feel quite conversant with the Special Educational Needs Code of Practice (2002). However, you may be less familiar with other statutory requirements. The important expression in Standard 2.1 relates to 'frameworks relevant to their role'. There will not be an expectation that you know every piece of educational legislation, but assessors will expect that you can demonstrate an understanding of those which have a direct bearing upon your professional performance.

In the publication *Guidance to the Standards* (TTA 2004b) it was noted that

> *Support staff meeting this standard will be able to demonstrate they are aware of the legal framework that underpins teaching and learning, and broader support and protection for both pupils and adults. Whilst it is not necessary to for them to have a detailed knowledge of the whole legal framework they will be aware of their statutory responsibilities and where to gain information, support and assistance when they need it.* (p. 17)

There are, of course, policies and statutes, which relate to critical elements such as child protection, of which all professionals working in schools need to have a good working knowledge.

Some standards contain a number of composite statements, for example Standard 1.1:

> *They have high expectations of all pupils; respect their social, cultural, linguistic, religious and ethnic backgrounds; and are committed to raising their educational achievement.*

It may be that you work in a situation where there are few, or indeed no children for whom English is an additional language, and that there is little cultural diversity within your school. This cannot to be taken as a reason for not being aware of your responsibilities or for demonstrating your ability to meet this particular standard. It is quite possible that in the future the nature of your school population may change or that having gained your HLTA status you move to a different school with a more diverse population. It is therefore important that you demonstrate that you can meet this standard in full.

Other standards may be specific to your working situation in other ways. For example, Standard 2.2 states that:

They are familiar with the school curriculum, the age-related expectations of pupils, the main teaching methods and the testing/examination frameworks in the subjects and age ranges in which they are involved.

If you are working in a junior school it is to be expected that you are familiar with the requirements of the National Curriculum for pupils working in Key Stage 2. However, it would be reasonable to expect you to have some understanding of the requirements and content from the National Curriculum at both Key Stages 1 and 3 as there may be pupils in your school who as a result of special educational needs or being gifted or talented may be working outside of the programmes of study for their chronological age. In some instances, in your role as a TA you may be supporting pupils in a specific area of the curriculum such as literacy or numeracy and have little input into other subject based lessons. You will, however, be expected to demonstrate an understanding of broader curriculum requirements in respect of the age range with which you are working.

Familiarity with the standards is essential if you are to succeed in providing sufficient evidence to go through the assessment process. You should make full use of the *Guidance to the Standards* document, which will clarify interpretation of these and provides some useful exemplars. It is equally important that you seek the advice of experienced colleagues in your school who may be able to provide clarification with regards to school policies and point you in the direction of useful information.

The HLTA Standards are demanding and it would therefore be surprising if you did not find that you needed to improve your work in relation to some of these. This book is intended to provide a broad overview which will assist you in attaining the standards, but cannot act as a substitute for your own efforts in gaining information through your school and by engaging in professional conversation with your colleagues. Clearly, if you are undertaking training related to the HLTA you should receive guidance and support from your tutors. However, as stated in the assessment principles, it is anticipated that you will keep your own detailed records in support of the assessment process.

Summary

- There are three main routes into HLTA and you need to consider carefully which is most appropriate for you.
- The support of your school and colleagues is essential in enabling you to make a smooth progress through this process.
- In order to achieve HLTA status you will need to complete a series of assessments which indicate that you have achieved the standards.

References

Department for Education and Skills (2002) *Special Educational Needs Code of Practice*. London: DfES.

Teacher Training Agency (2004a) *Professional Standards for Higher Level Teaching Assistants*. London: TTA.

Teacher Training Agency (2004b) *Meeting the Professional Standards for the Award of the Higher Level Teaching Assistant Status: Guidance to the Standards*. London TTA.

2. Statutory frameworks

Introduction

Teaching assistants have come to play a significant role in supporting the education of pupils with SEN in mainstream schools. (Thomas 1992)

As a professional TA you will be aware of the wide diversity of experience, strengths, needs and motivations in the pupils that you teach and support. How then do we define 'special needs'? Frederickson and Cline (2002) draw attention to a distinction between the special needs that may be experienced by particular groups of children whose circumstances or background differ from the majority of children; for example, children for whom the language of instruction is not the same as that used at home, children in public care, or individual children who have learning difficulties and require special educational services.

A historical perspective on how government laws and policies have shaped SEN practice will help develop your understanding of how special educational needs have come to be defined, the values that underpin current thinking about SEN and appreciation of the importance of effective teaching and learning strategies in meeting the needs of all learners.

An overview of the legislation and reports of the last 60 years shows there have been significant changes in thinking about SEN in terms of:

- how SEN is defined
- where pupils with SEN are educated
- how pupils with SEN are taught.

HLTA STANDARDS

1.1 They have high expectations of all pupils; respect their social, cultural, linguistic, religious and ethnic backgrounds; and are committed to raising their educational achievement.

1.4 They work collaboratively with colleagues, and carry out their roles effectively, knowing when to seek help and advice.

1.5 They are able to liaise sensitively with parents and carers, recognising their roles in pupils' learning.

2.1 They have sufficient understanding of their specialist area to support pupils' learning, and are able to acquire further knowledge to contribute effectively and with confidence to the classes in which they are involved. (If SEN specialist area.)

2.7   They are aware of the statutory frameworks relevant to their role.

2.8   They know the legal definition of Special Educational Needs (SEN) and are familiar with the guidance about meeting SEN given in the SEN Code of Practice.

3.3.3 They promote and support the inclusion of all pupils in the learning activities in which they are involved.

CHAPTER OBJECTIVES

This chapter considers how teachers and TAs working together can respond to the current legislation and advice governing special educational needs in order to promote inclusive classrooms. Cross-references within the text will direct the reader to chapters which explore the issues raised in more depth.

By the end of this chapter you should:

● have a basic knowledge and understanding of the legislation relating to SEN and inclusion

● know the ways in which your school responds to this legislation

● be familiar with the SEN policy for your school

● have considered what the legislation means for you as a TA supporting pupils with special educational needs.

How do we define special educational needs?

It was not until 1970, with the passing of the Education (Mentally Handicapped Children) Act, that pupils with learning difficulties became entitled to receive an education. Prior to this act, pupils with severe or profound and multiple learning difficulties were described as 'ineducable', and accommodated in hospitals under the responsibility of the Health Service.

The Warnock Report of 1978 was an important landmark in developing people's thinking about what constitutes SEN. It introduced a wider definition of 'special educational needs' to include not just those pupils with significant special needs educated in special schools but all pupils and young persons whose educational needs could not be met by the classroom teacher without some help.

This report reflected a new thinking that moved away from a medical diagnosis of disability to identifying special educational needs. The term 'SEN' was introduced in the Education Act (1981) to replace the previous list of disabilities of mind and body used in the 1944 Act (e.g. descriptions such as 'educationally sub-normal' (ESN) and 'maladjusted').

The 1981 Act definition of SEN was used in the 1993 and 1996 Education Acts:

A child has a special education need if s/he has a learning difficulty which calls for special educational needs provision to be made for him or her. A child has a learning difficulty if s/he:

- *has a significantly greater difficulty in learning than the majority of children of the same age, or*
- *has a disability which prevents or hinders the child from making use of educational facilities of the kind provided for children of the same age in schools within the area of the Local Education Authority (LEA).*
- *Pupils who speak English an additional language should not be considered as having SEN for this reason alone.*

The Education Act (1981) also introduced legally binding statements of special educational need for some pupils which committed LEAs to providing resources for an individual pupil, in a mainstream setting wherever possible.

Although the 1981 Act set out principles that should encourage high expectations of all pupils regardless of needs or ability, in practice, defining SEN in terms of the resources needed to support individual pupils has been a double-edged sword. Moore (1999) talks of the 'perverse incentive' where schools can be thought of as being rewarded with additional resources for demonstrating persistent lack of achievement.

In addition, the process of referral for statutory assessment for statements of special educational need could lead to a focus of attention on the pupil's ability to access the education provided, rather than also looking at factors within the school environment which may act as barriers to pupils' efficient learning. For example, a pupil with emotional, social and behavioural difficulties can thrive in a setting where social skills are taught and effective behaviour-management strategies are in place in one year, and struggle in a setting where behaviour-management strategies are less clear and consistent during another year.

Where do we educate pupils with special educational needs?

The Warnock Report proposed the integration of pupils into local mainstream schools wherever possible, suggesting that it was wrong to categorise pupils by means of their handicap and send them to special schools. The focus should instead be on identifying their educational difficulties and making appropriate provision accordingly. Provision 'wherever possible' should occur within mainstream practice.

The Education Act of 1993 and 1996 confirmed the general principle that pupils with SEN should – where this is what parents wanted – normally be educated at mainstream schools. However, pupils and their families had to satisfy a series of conditions: the mainstream's ability to ensure the pupil received the educational provision his or her learning difficulty called for while also ensuring the efficient education of other pupils and the efficient use of resources. The SEN and Disability Act of 2001 strengthened a pupil's right to a mainstream education.

From integration to inclusion

Although the principle of integration had been established, successful integration depended on the pupil's ability to adapt to an unchanged school environment. Focusing on the needs of pupils with SEN prevented schools from addressing the issue referred to earlier: the factors within the school and the classroom which may act as barriers to all pupils' efficient learning.

The language began to change, reflecting a new perspective on how to educate pupils with SEN. People began to talk about 'inclusion' rather than 'integration' and to focus on schools wider purpose: the creation of an inclusive society:

> Mainstream schools are the most effective means of ... building an inclusive society and achieving education for all. (UNESCO 'Salamanca' Statement 1994)

This encapsulates the notion of 'social inclusion' which is concerned with a pupil's right to belong to their local mainstream school, within a neighbourhood school community that accepts and values difference.

The government green paper *Excellence for all Children* (1997) outlined ideas for the development of inclusive education: inclusion of all in mainstream schools and redefining the role of special schools. This has led to a focus not on *where* we educate pupils with SEN but on *how* we educate pupils with SEN.

How do we educate pupils with special educational needs?

Current educational thinking encourages us to focus less on the perceived special educational needs of individuals and more on eliminating barriers to learning within the school environment, e.g. values and attitudes, management, organisation, learning and teaching styles. Inclusion has come to be seen as an integral part of school improvement which understands that effective teaching and learning strategies benefit all pupils. Refer to Chapters 5 and 6 for a discussion of access strategies and teaching and learning styles.

One of the principles for learning and teaching in *Excellence and Enjoyment* includes: 'demonstrating a commitment to every learner's success, making them feel included, valued and secure' (DfES 2004b). The Education Reform Act (1988) initiated the process when it stated that *all* pupils are entitled to access the National Curriculum (NC) which is 'broad and balanced'. It stated that special schools have to follow the National Curriculum.

The National Curriculum Inclusion Statement (1999) set out three principles essential to developing a more inclusive curriculum:

- setting suitable learning challenges
- responding to pupils' diverse learning needs
- overcoming potential barriers to learning and assessment for individuals and groups of pupils.

These three principles are referred to as 'the three principles of inclusion' and inform and are repeated in recent curriculum documents published by the DfES. (See Chapters 4, 5 and 6 for information about how to apply these principles in the classroom.)

As a professional TA supporting pupils with SEN, you need, in particular, to be aware of the requirements of the SEN Code of Practice (2001) and the Special Educational Needs and Disability Act (2001).

The Special Educational Needs Code of Practice (2001)

This replaced the earlier Code of Practice (1994) and set out the responsibilities of LEAs, schools and individual teachers for the management of pupils with SEN. It is subject to inspection by Ofsted.

The document contains separate chapters on provision in the early years, primary and secondary phases, and new chapters on:

- working partnership with parents
- pupil participation
- working in partnership with other agencies.

(Chapters 8 and 9 of this book explore pupil participation and effective partnership working.)

The Code of Practice sets out a graduated approach to the assessment and planning for pupils with SEN. It does this through the identification and implementation of stages of assessment and the identification of actions to be taken by schools through School Action and School Action Plus or (in the case of pupils in the early years) through Early Years Action and Early Years Action Plus. In a minority of cases pupils may be given a statement of special educational needs, which is a statutory document recognising that pupils' needs cannot be met by using the resources normally available within the school, and setting out how provision will be organised.

The fundamental principles are that:

- a pupil with SEN should have their needs met and be offered full access to a broad and balanced education, including an appropriate curriculum for the Foundation stage and the National Curriculum
- the SEN of pupils will normally be met in mainstream or early education settings
- the views of the pupil should be sought and taken into account
- parents have a vital role to play in supporting their child's education.

These principles should underpin the school's SEN policy and practice. As a professional TA who is likely to be supporting pupils with SEN, these are also the principles that should inform the work that you do.

PRACTICAL TASK

Look at the school's SEN policy and familiarise yourself with its content:

- school procedures for identifying special educational needs
- how information is gathered and communicated
- the roles and responsibilities of the SENCo, class teacher and professional TA in supporting pupils with SEN
- how parents are informed and involved in their child's education
- how staff are supported and trained to meet SEN
- the name of the Special Needs Governor and how s/he acts on behalf of the governing body to monitor the SEN policy
- outside agencies with whom the school works, including named personnel.

Early identification

The Code of Practice offers guidance on how to ensure that pupils with special educational needs are identified early. It suggests that the key for a school to take action is recognising that the current rate of progress being made by the pupils is inadequate. It is therefore important for schools to have clear systems for monitoring the progress of pupils, for example, by referring to:

- their performance monitored by the teacher as part of ongoing observation and assessment
- information from Foundation stage profile
- their progress against the objectives specified in the NLS and NNS Frameworks
- their performance against the level descriptions within the National Curriculum, at the end of a key stage
- standardised screening or assessment tools (5:13) (refer to Chapter 7 for information about assessment).

As a professional TA you can assist this process by informing the teacher of any concerns that you have and by keeping your own records of how pupils respond to activities or tasks which you manage:

> the truth which seems to have emerged is that for all children, the best way to assess them is quite simply, to look at what they are doing and talk to them about it...   (Thomas and Loxley 2001, p. 26)

Case study

Gloria is a TA in a Year 4 class in a junior school. She is supporting a group working on real-life money problem-solving questions by reading questions to them; role-playing handling coins; visual support using number lines; and whiteboards to record their thinking. She notices that Leona in a different group is getting upset because she doesn't understand the questions. She quietly suggests that she joins her group, offers her reassurance and helps her to complete the work independently by explaining and modelling problem-solving strategies using concrete materials and role play.

After the session she explains to the teacher why Leona was upset and the action she has taken to enable her to complete the task. Gloria and the teacher discuss the need to use practical activities to support pupils' understanding and how they will plan them into future lessons. Gloria and the teacher also agree to monitor and support Leona's understanding through the use of differentiated questioning.

Assessment of special needs

Difficulties in learning often arise from an unsuitable environment – inappropriate grouping of pupils, inflexible teaching styles, or inaccessible curriculum materials – as much as from individual children's physical, sensory or cognitive impairments. (DfES 2004a, p. 28)

The process of assessment advocated in the Special Educational Needs Code of Practice (2001, 5:6) reflects a view of SEN which believes the level of need to be the result of a complex interaction between within pupils' characteristics (learning style, unique pattern of strengths and weaknesses) and the environment in which they are being taught. The Code of Practice advises a four-fold approach to assessment that looks at the interplay between the individual pupil's learning characteristics, the environment in which they are being educated, the work that they are required to do and the way that they are taught.

PUPIL'S LEARNING CHARACTERISTICS	LEARNING ENVIRONMENT
(e.g. learning style, motivation, persistence, attention control, independence, concentration, social skills, literacy skills, understanding, numeracy skills)	(e.g. room size, light, temperature, noise level, displays, resource availability and management, rules and routines, staffing, seating and grouping arrangements)
THE TASK	**TEACHING STYLE**
(e.g. individual, paired, group, adult support, time span, investigation, discussion, role play, planning, writing, drawing, reading, constructing, using ICT)	(e.g. sharing lesson objectives, explaining, questioning, demonstrating, modelling, use of ICT, feedback to pupils, reviewing lesson)

Identify a pupil that is having difficulties with learning. Record brief bullet-point notes under each of the headings in the above grid. Observe how they respond to teaching and learning in different lessons and at different times of the day and week, using the headings in the grid.

- What do you notice about the relationship between their individual learning characteristics and the classroom environment?
- What helps them to learn?
- What hinders their learning?

Adequate progress

The Code of Practice states: 'There should not be an assumption that all children will progress at the same rate.' Defining what constitutes 'adequate progress' is difficult. The Code of Practice (5: 42, p. 52) offers some indicators of adequate progress:

- closes the attainment gap between the pupil and his/her peers
- prevents the attainment gap growing wider
- is similar to that of peers starting from the same attainment level but less than that of the majority of their peers
- progress matches or betters the pupil's previous rate of progress
- ensures full access to the curriculum
- demonstrates an improvement in self-help, social or personal skills
- demonstrates improvements in behaviour.

Early Years Action and School Action

When a pupil is not making adequate progress, the teacher will normally consult the school's SENCo. The triggers for School Action are when the pupil is:

- making little or no progress despite areas of weakness being targeted (for example, through the Wave 2 literacy and numeracy interventions: Early Literacy Support (ELS), Additional Literacy Support (ALS) or Further Literacy Support (FLS) or the Springboard maths programmes)
- showing signs of difficulty in developing literacy or mathematical skills with poor attainment in some curriculum areas
- presenting persistent emotional, social, behavioural difficulties which are not managed or improved by behaviour management strategies
- experiencing sensory/physical difficulties and making little or no progress despite provision of equipment
- showing persistent communication/interaction difficulties.

If through the observation and assessments made, and discussion with the SENCo, it is believed that the pupil will not learn unless interventions are made which are additional to or different from those which the teacher normally provides in class, then there may be a decision to proceed to Early Years Action or School Action.

'Additional to and different from' means a pupil needs an individual teaching approach/strategy leading to a different outcome from the rest of the class. ELS and ALS (when used within the cohort for whom they are intended) are examples of appropriate differentiation and are not 'additional to and different from'.

The strategies to be used to assist a pupil in making progress should be incorporated in an individual education plan (IEP). TAs often have a key role in implementing an IEP but the teacher remains responsible for the planning, assessing and monitoring of the programme. Sometimes it may be decided with the parents' consent to involve professionals from outside the school and the TA may play a key role in gathering and providing evidence.

Early Years Action Plus and School Action Plus

If the pupil continues to make little or no progress, despite the actions of the school through School Action, then the SENCo and class teacher, in consultation with parents, may ask for help from other agencies, e.g. educational psychologist, health professionals, behaviour support team.

These professionals may be asked to conduct more detailed assessments or offer input into the development of specific programmes. Additional or different strategies are put in place and recorded on a new IEP.

The role of the TA is one of support to the pupil and to the parent. S/he can continue to collate information and share observations and ideas with professional colleagues.

Case study

Alisha is a TA in a reception class. She attends a pre-school review meeting at a nursery for Molly, a child with mild autistic difficulties. Molly has been supported at Early Years Action Plus and parents are anxious about her impending transfer to school.

At this meeting it is agreed that Molly will attend all the taster sessions to allow her extra time to get to know the staff and the school environment. Furthermore, Molly will be in the first cohort of pupils to join the Reception class in September, to allow her time to settle in before the whole class is in full-time. Parents and nursery staff share effective strategies for teaching and supporting Molly to ensure continuity and consistency and a successful transition to school. Alisha maintains informal contact with the parents throughout the transition period and beyond, describing and recording Molly's activities achievements in a home-school diary to which the parents also contribute.

> *Alisha invites the parents and the specialist support teacher from the LEA to a post-transition meeting. The minutes of the meeting record how Molly has settled well into school, detail the progress she has made and that parents are very happy with the way the transition has been organised.*

This case study illustrates how the principles underpinning the Code of Practice have informed the support given to Molly and her parents. Molly's needs have been identified at the pre-school stage and a specialist support teacher, nursery staff and parents have worked together to ensure the maintenance of consistent behaviour-management strategies and to provide opportunities for her to develop communication and social skills within a structured environment. Support needs have been anticipated, monitored and evaluated throughout the transition period. Early intervention and effective partnerships with parents and outside agencies have ensured that Molly has settled well into her new school.

Statutory assessment

In some cases, it will be necessary for schools to seek statutory assessment of a pupil which may result in a statement of special educational needs being issued. This involves the LEA, working co-operatively with parents, the pupil's school and other agencies, as appropriate, deciding whether a statutory assessment of the pupil's educational needs is necessary. The LEA will seek evidence from the school that strategies and programmes implemented over a period of time have been unsuccessful:

- the school's action through Early Years/School Action or Early Years/School Action Plus
- individual education plans (IEPs) for the pupil
- records of reviews and their outcomes
- pupil's health including medical history where relevant
- National Curriculum levels
- attainment in literacy and mathematics
- educational and other assessments
- views of the parents and of the pupil
- involvement of other professionals
- any involvement of social services or education welfare service.

The description of the pupil's learning difficulty and progress, with information about any specialist provision made, will form the basis on which the LEA considers the necessity of a statutory assessment. Statutory assessment does not always lead to a statement.

Statement of special educational needs

A statement sets out long-term objectives, provision, monitoring arrangements and placement for pupil plus any non-educational needs and provision. All statements are reviewed annually when parents, pupil, school, LEA and other professionals involved, monitor and evaluate continued effectiveness and relevance of provision being made.

SEN and Disability Act (2001)

In order to meet their responsibilities towards pupils with SEN, all schools must have due regard to the SEN and Disability Act (2001) (SENDA). This amended the Disability Discrimination Act (1995) from September 2002, creating important new duties:

- For schools and many early years settings to take 'reasonable steps' to ensure that disabled pupils are not placed at a substantial disadvantage in relation to the education and other services they provide. This means that they must anticipate where barriers to learning lie and take action to remove them as far as they are able.

- For schools, most early years settings and LEAs to plan strategically to increase the extent to which disabled pupils can participate in the curriculum, make the physical environment more accessible and ensure that written information is provided in accessible formats.

- A pupil who has SEN and a statement must be educated in a mainstream school unless this would be incompatible with the wishes of the parents or the provision of efficient education of other pupils:

  A parent's wish to have their learner with a statement educated in the mainstream should only be refused in the small minority of cases where the child's inclusion would be incompatible with the efficient education of other children. (DfES 2001b, 1:35, p. 14)

Inclusive Schooling: Children with Special Educational Needs (DfES 2001a)

This provides statutory guidance on the practical operation of the framework for inclusion. It includes examples of reasonable steps schools might take to ensure the inclusion of pupils with a range of special needs. For example, it suggests that the reasonable steps to include a primary aged pupil who has severe temper tantrums may include:

- addressing factors within the class that may be contributing to the problem, e.g. teasing, by using circle time as a forum for discussing teasing and how to respond to it
- teaching the pupil alternative behaviours, e.g. taking quiet time in a specially designated area

- drawing up a contingency plan for what will happen if there is a confrontation in class
- ensuring that if there is any possibility that positive handling may need to be used to prevent injury to others or to property, that relevant staff have had training in appropriate techniques, that these have been carefully explained to the pupil, and that the circumstances under which they may be used have been recorded on a written plan agreed with and signed by the pupil and his or her parents/carers.

TAs have an important role in identifying barriers to inclusion and in offering creative solutions to enable pupils with a range of difficulties to participate in different learning situations, including out of school contexts.

Case study

Jacob, in a mainstream school, has a statement for social and communication difficulties associated with autistic spectrum disorder. In the past he has had temper tantrums which have been triggered by unwanted changes in routine although the frequency and severity of these incidents is greatly reduced. The class teacher has concerns about including the boy in a planned visit to a local theatre as he might pose a threat to the safety and well-being of other pupils and the public.

The class teacher and the TA, David, conduct a risk assessment for the visit. With careful preparation and sufficient adult support, there is no justification for not including Jacob in the visit. They draw up a contingency plan to cover any potential temper tantrums. David liaises with the parents and both spend some time preparing Jacob for the visit, including the writing of a social story and drawing up a visual timetable.

On the day of the visit David ensures Jacob is paired up with a friend with whom he feels comfortable, talks them through the routine and observes carefully for any signs of anxiety or distress. The visit proceeds smoothly and without incident.

In this situation the teacher and TA have used a risk assessment which is a starting point for any out-of-school visit. On the basis of an assessment of the risks posed by taking Jacob with them, they conclude that Jacob should participate in the visit. By making reasonable adjustments, which include preparing Jacob for the visit, ensuring sufficient adult support and having a contingency plan, Jacob is able to be included in the visit to the theatre.

Summary

The change in the language used over the years from 'ineducable' and, 'handicapped', through 'integration', to 'inclusion' and 'removing barriers to achievement' illustrates a change in attitude towards pupils with SEN. While it is not necessary to have an in-depth knowledge of the statutory frameworks related to SEN and inclusion, it is important to understand how the legislation informs the work that you do in working with teachers to support pupils and their parents/carers in terms of:

- early identification of pupils with SEN
- assessing the needs of pupils with SEN
- making provision for pupils with SEN in the context of an inclusive curriculum which is based on the National Curriculum three principles of inclusion.

References

Department for Education and Employment (1996) *Education Act*. London: DfEE.

Department for Education and Employment (2001) *Special Educational Needs and Disability Act*. London: The Stationery Office.

Department for Education and Skills (2001a) *Inclusive Schooling: Children with Special Educational Needs*. London: DfES.

Department for Education and Skills (2001b) *Special Educational Needs Code of Practice*. London: DfES.

Department for Education and Skills (2004a) *Removing Barriers to Achievement: The Government's Strategy for SEN*. London: DfES.

Department for Education and Skills (2004b) *Excellence and Enjoyment: Learning and Teaching in the Primary Years*. London: DfES.

Frederickson, N. and Cline, T. (2002) *Special Educational Needs, Inclusion and Diversity: a Textbook*. Buckingham: Open University Press.

Moore, J. (1999) Developing a local authority responsibility to inclusion. *Support for Learning*, 14(4): 174–8.

Quicke, J. (2003) Educating the pupil voice. *Support for Learning*, 18 (2): 51–57.

Thomas, G. (1992) *Effective Classroom Teamwork: Support or Intrusion?* London: Routledge.

Thomas, G. and Loxley, A. (2001) *Deconstructing Special Education and Constructing Inclusion*. Buckingham: Open University Press.

3. Individual education plans

Introduction

Some pupils do not make adequate progress in the key areas of cognition and learning, communication and interaction, and behavioural, emotional and social development; or their sensory or physical needs act as a significant barrier to participation and progress in their learning.

An individual education plan (IEP) is an assessment, planning, teaching and reviewing tool which records specific learning goals, teaching requirements and review arrangements, to help a pupil with SEN which are 'additional to and different from' those of most pupils, to make progress in the key areas of learning. It is important to focus on the process; the IEP document itself is a record of that process.

As a professional TA, you are likely to have an important role to play in the whole process of an IEP: assessment, planning, teaching and review. This will involve you in working with the pupil, parents, teachers and other professionals to identify individual needs, gather information, establish priority areas for learning, set targets, implement programmes and monitor and evaluate progress.

HLTA STANDARDS

1.1   They have high expectations of all pupils; respect their social, cultural, linguistic, religious and ethnic backgrounds; and are committed to raising their educational achievement.

1.4   They work collaboratively with colleagues, and carry out their roles effectively, knowing when to seek help and advice.

1.5   They are able to liaise sensitively and effectively with parents and carers, recognising their roles in pupils' learning.

2.1   They have sufficient understanding of their specialist area to support pupils' learning, and are able to acquire further knowledge to contribute effectively and with confidence to the classes in which they are involved.

2.2   They are familiar with the school curriculum, the age-related expectations of pupils, the main teaching methods and the testing/examination frameworks in the subjects and age ranges in which they are involved.

2.4   They know how to use ICT to advance pupils' learning, and can use common ICT tools for their own and pupils' benefit.

2.5   They know the key factors that can affect the way pupils learn.

▶

HLTA STANDARDS

2.7   They are aware of the statutory frameworks relevant to their role.

2.8   They know the legal definition of special educational needs (SEN), and are familiar with the guidance about meeting SEN given in the SEN Code of Practice.

3.1.1   They contribute effectively to teachers' planning and preparation of lessons.

3.2.1   They are able to support teachers in evaluating pupils' progress through a range of assessment activities.

3.2.2   They monitor pupils' responses to learning tasks and modify their approach accordingly.

3.2.3   They monitor pupils' participation and progress, providing feedback to teachers, and giving constructive support to pupils as they learn.

3.2.4   They contribute to maintaining and analysing records of pupils' progress.

3.3.1   Using clearly structured teaching and learning activities, they interest and motivate pupils, and advance their learning.

3.3.2   They communicate effectively and sensitively with pupils to support their learning.

3.3.5   They advance pupils' learning in a range of classroom settings, including working with individuals ... small groups...

CHAPTER OBJECTIVES

By the end of this chapter you should understand how professional TAs working in collaboration with pupils, parents, teachers and other agencies can contribute to:

● identification of pupils whose rate of progress is a cause for concern

● gathering and collating of information to help identify priority areas for learning

● implementation of IEPs through teaching and support

● monitoring and evaluation of progress towards personal targets.

Levels of response to special educational needs

Schools should not assume that children's learning difficulties always result solely, or even mainly, from problems within the child. (Code of Practice 5:18)

The Code of Practice advises that there is a continuum of special educational needs and that special educational provision should be matched to a pupil's current educational needs.

A pupil's lack of progress can be due to gaps in their learning or the way they have been taught. This is why the SEN Code of Practice (2001a) describes a 'graduated response' to identifying and meeting SEN and why the National Literacy Strategy (NLS), National Numeracy Strategy (NNS) and Social and Emotional Aspects of Learning (SEAL) strategy describe the response to an individual's need in terms of 'waves' of support.

Wave One: this is described as 'quality first teaching' which ensures the inclusion of all pupils through the effective implementation of the National Curriculum, National Literacy Strategy, National Numeracy Strategy and whole-school behaviour management policy.

Wave Two: this refers to 'catch-up' programmes, for example, springboard maths, additional literacy support or social skills group interventions.

These are not SEN interventions and pupils do not require an IEP because they are on these programmes although they may have additional special needs for which they may need an IEP.

Wave Three: these are specific targeted approaches for individual pupils identified as requiring SEN intervention. The programmes or approaches might include the adjustment of learning objectives and teaching styles, and /or individual support which may draw on specialist advice.

Pupils receiving Wave Three support will need an IEP and will be placed on one of the following.

Early Years Action/School Action

This is where pupils' needs might be resolved by the resources and expertise available in school.

Early Years Action Plus/School Action Plus

This is where an external agency is involved in assessment, planning and review. For some pupils whose progress gives continued cause for concern, additional action may be needed, involving consultation with outside agencies, for example, the educational psychologist or speech and language therapist.

Triggers for School Action Plus are described in paragraph 5:56, p. 55, of the Code of Practice:

- Continues to make little or no progress in specific areas over a long period.
- Continues working at National Curriculum levels substantially below that expected of pupils of a similar age.
- Continues to have difficulties in developing literacy and mathematics skills.

- Has emotional and behavioural difficulties which substantially and regularly interfere with the pupil's own learning or that of the class group, despite having an individualised behaviour management programme.
- Has sensory or physical needs, and requires additional specialist equipment or regular advice or visits by a specialist service.
- Has an ongoing communication or interaction difficulty that impedes the development of social relationships and cause substantial barriers to learning.

Including all Children in the Literacy Hour and Daily Mathematics Lesson (DfES 2002) and 'Strands of action to meet SEN' from the *SEN Toolkit* (DfES 2001b) summarise the types of provision appropriate to each wave of support.

The IEP is, therefore, for pupils who have needs which cannot be met through the 'waves' of provision, One and Two. They have individual needs which are 'additional to' or 'different from' those of most pupils.

PRACTICAL TASK

Many schools are developing school provision maps which record the different types of provision made for pupils within the school.

Discuss the different types of provision available to pupils within the year group or class you support with the SENCo and/or class teacher. Try mapping the different types of provision made for pupils working at and below age expectation in the class or classes you support. Some examples have been provided to support your understanding of the task.

AREA OF NEED	WAVE ONE	WAVE TWO	EARLY YEARS/ SCHOOL ACTION	EARLY YEARS/ SCHOOL ACTION PLUS
Cognition and learning		e.g. Early Literacy Support/ Additional Literacy Support programmes to help groups of learners 'catch up' with peers	e.g. Primary National Strategy: 'Wave 3 Mathematics' individualised programme focusing on a pupil's specific difficulty	

AREA OF NEED	WAVE ONE	WAVE TWO	EARLY YEARS/ SCHOOL ACTION	EARLY YEARS/ SCHOOL ACTION PLUS
Communication and interaction		Social skills group to improve social interaction in unstructured times		TA implements pragmatic skills programme for named pupil in group setting, under guidance of a speech and language therapist
Emotional, behavioural and social	e.g. Whole-school behaviour policy and reward scheme			
Sensory and physical				e.g. Daily 10 min physiotherapy programme with TA working under guidance of the physiotherapist

What is an effective IEP?

The IEP document contains teaching and learning plans setting out the knowledge, understanding and skills which should be taught through additional or different activities from those provided for all pupils through the differentiated curriculum. It is used to plan the interventions for individual pupils made through Early Years Action or Early Years Action Plus; School Action and School Action Plus; and for pupils with statements of SEN.

Establishing priority needs

Targets in IEPs focus on the current prioritised individual needs of a pupil within the context of the curriculum. Information is obtained about a pupil's stage of development, their strengths and needs, their interests, their favoured learning style, responses to teaching style, optimum learning environment, and support they need to learn most effectively. Although this information does not form part of the IEP, teachers and TAs will need to refer to the individual record or pupil profile which contains information about a pupil's particular needs, current strengths and support or management protocols.

Case study

Example of a pupil at School Action Plus

Priority needs to be addressed on an IEP

Martin is a Year 2 boy with behavioural and emotional difficulties which substantially and regularly interfere with his learning and occasionally that of the class group. His behaviour is thought to reflect difficult and unsettled home circumstances. He will often refuse to comply with adult instructions either because he doesn't think he can do a task or because he doesn't want to. This is particularly noticeable when he has to move from an activity he is enjoying to a directed task. Initially he will ignore instructions or simply not comply but this behaviour can quickly escalate into full-blown tantrums.

Other needs to be met within normal classroom differentiation

Martin is expected to participate in all class activities which are differentiated. He has access to Helen, a TA, if required, under class teacher direction.

He is receiving 20 minutes daily phonics teaching in a group of five and individual reading practice with Helen.

The whole class does regular circle time activities focusing on speaking and listening skills and recognising and managing feelings. Helen includes Martin in a smaller circle for part of the circle time to enable Martin to receive more attention than would be possible in the larger class circle.

Teaching strategies and materials

Martin likes encouragement, frequent specific positive feedback and stickers.

He prefers to link in with the School Behaviour Plan whereby every child earns a tick for a good day, so the individual monitoring sheet has been discontinued.

He likes his 'Terrific' book in which positive comments are recorded at home and at school.

Helen has observed that Martin shows early warning signs of stress by pulling his own hair or ears, scratching his face, and growling and squealing. She and the teacher have noted that prompt early intervention can sometimes prevent his behaviour escalating into a tantrum.

The tactics they use are to give Martin a warning of changes in activities and providing short multi-sensory activities, breaking them up into small steps.

The next level of intervention is the use of 'think time' when Martin and Helen move to a 'safe place' in the library where he can use his 'Happy book/Happy key ring'. Occasionally, in spite of these preventative measures, Martin loses his temper and will kick the tables and throw objects around the room.

If this happens, a help card will be sent to the office to trigger help and the class will be moved out into the shared area.

Once Martin is calm again, he likes to tidy up. He may ask to draw a picture to express his feelings. He likes to make amends and in the past has apologised to the class and invited them to return to the room.

Helen is then able to talk about what happened and uses cartoons/story/think sheets to help Martin think about what he could have done differently.

Preparing an IEP with Martin

Helen talks to Martin and he tells her that he likes:

- *drawing, colouring and painting and feels that he is good at these activities*
- *playing with his friends*
- *looking at books and magazines.*

He doesn't like writing because it is hard work but he agrees that it helps to have a short task to do and to be able to draw a picture to illustrate it.

He doesn't like losing his temper because it makes him cry afterwards. He would like to be able to stop himself before it happens. They discuss how the adults can help him use his key ring and happy book to calm him down.

'If I feel angry I will take my key ring out of my pocket and walk with an adult to the library. I will look at my happy book to help me calm down.'

Helen then records Martin's target: It is to follow adult instructions, accepting guidance and support from adults when he is upset.

This is a behaviour and learning management plan for a pupil at School Action Plus. The priority need is to eliminate the episodes where Martin loses self-control and the target and arrangements on his IEP reflect this need.

Martin has other needs – for example, in writing tasks – but other pupils in the class also need help to start a writing task and require modelling and small-step instructions, so whole-class planning needs to take this issue into consideration.

Priority needs and appropriate strategies have been established in discussion with the pupil and parent, and consultation with the educational psychologist. The TA and teacher have worked together to collate and record the information to inform the targets and to ensure consistent management of Martin's behaviour and learning.

Short-term targets set for or by the pupil

These are usually in the key areas of communication, literacy, mathematics and aspects of behaviour or physical skills, which would not otherwise be met through the teacher's whole-class planning. It is important to remember that the IEP is designed to address the pupil's current priority needs and that the pupil should still be offered the full National Curriculum. The IEP 'should be crisply written' (Code of Practice 5:51) and should only record the targets that are 'additional to or different from' (5:51) those in place for the rest of the group or class.

Inclusive educational practice is fostered when individual needs are considered in the context of whole-class teaching and learning so target-setting should identify opportunities within curriculum provision for individual needs to be addressed:

> schools need to give greater attention not so much to the specific details of the IEP, but to how it relates to the teacher's planning.   (Ofsted 1997)

They need to be achievable targets for both the pupil and the teacher. The acronym SMART is used in the Code of Practice to define an appropriate target.

SMART targets

SMART targets are phrased in terms of what a pupil will do as a result of a particular intervention or strategy.

Specific
This means that the target is specific to the identified priority needs of the pupil and is additional to whole class targets.

Measurable
Changes in skills, knowledge and understanding are observable and staff and pupils will be able to judge when the target has been met.

Achievable
Targets are based on a sound knowledge of the pupil's current levels of achievement *and* rate of learning. They are challenging but also realistic for the pupil in the time and context.

Relevant
The targets address important priorities for the pupil and relate to their needs in the whole curriculum. They do not isolate the pupil from their peers.

Time bound
A review date has been set.

Examples of SMART targets

TARGET	SUCCESS CRITERIA
Ahmed can use initial sounds to help him work out a word he doesn't know	Reading miscue analysis shows Ahmed using phonics as one of his strategies to decode unknown words
Micky can transfer spelling of taught high-frequency words to independent writing in the classroom	Analysis of writing tasks in exercise books shows that Micky is spelling or self-correcting words accurately
Lauren can understand and use prepositions 'in front of' and 'behind' to describe positions of objects and people	Lauren shows understanding and use when assessed in different settings (e.g. playground, PE and maths) on at least three random occasions

Note how opportunities to demonstrate achievement have been identified within daily classroom activities as well as in formal assessment activities.

Pupil contribution to IEPs

The new Code of Practice makes it very clear that pupils should be involved in planning their targets from an early age and that they should become progressively more involved as they develop and mature, without overburdening them.

> *Children and young people should where possible participate in all the decision making processes that occur in education. They should feel confident that they will be listened to and that their views are valued.* (SEN Code of Practice 3.2)

Engaging pupils in setting targets, discovering the strategies that help them learn and monitoring progress are important in developing their self-esteem. In practical terms this process means finding the space and the time to talk to pupils about their targets and to monitor their progress. As a professional TA you may be asked to contribute to this process.

Principles for involving pupils in target-setting

Working with very young children, pupils who have difficulties in the areas of language and communication and with those pupils who have never had the opportunity to express choices, can make the setting and monitoring of targets a challenging experience. Byers and Rose (2004) identify a number of principles for involving pupils in the target-setting process:

- *Involve pupils in choice and decision making from the earliest stages of schooling.*

- *Discuss pupils' targets with them regularly in order to keep these at the forefront of their attention.*

- *Ensure that pupils are aware of how they are doing in making progress towards the achievement of targets: visual representations such as progress charts can help.*

- *Find the most appropriate means of communicating with individual pupils and use these approaches consistently.*

- *Avoid involving pupils in too many targets – in some cases a single target may be appropriate.*

(Byers and Rose 2004, pp. 109–110)

Before negotiating targets with a pupil it is important to have an informal discussion about the activities a pupil likes and feels good at and those activities which the pupil does not like and feels bothered about. You can also share your own observations and information about priority areas of need. It is important to help the pupil to identify the things they would like to get better at, as the more closely the IEP targets mirror their own priorities, the more motivated they will be to work at achieving them.

'Enabling Pupil Participation' (*SEN Toolkit*) suggests that where possible, targets should be recorded in the pupil's own words or symbols, as in the following grid.

THINGS I WOULD LIKE TO GET BETTER AT	MY TARGETS	WHAT I WILL DO	PEOPLE WHO WILL HELP ME	I HOPE TO ACHIEVE THESE TARGETS BY DECEMBER 8TH
Telling the time	Read and set the time to the half hour [on an analogue clock]	I will take turns to read and set the clock with Mrs Brown. I will improve my score on the computer program	Mr Abbott and Mrs Brown. My friends will take turns with me to read and set the clock	
Handwriting	write letters 'b' and 'd' the right way round in my class work	I will use the 'bed' picture to remind me	Mrs Brown will give me a sticker each time she spots me checking	

Teaching strategies

It is very important to take into account the preferred learning styles, strengths and interests of the pupil. The pupil has failed to make adequate progress using the teaching strategies available to the whole class so they are likely to need something different in order to make progress.

Case study

Carl is in Year 1. He has generally poor co-ordination and follows an exercise programme set by a physiotherapist at home. He also has poor fine motor skills and is having great difficulty in forming his letters correctly.

Surinder, the TA, discusses Carl's fine motor skills with his class teacher and they agree that in order for Carl to achieve the target of writing his name independently, they need to consider alternative teaching techniques.

Using her knowledge of multi-sensory teaching techniques gained from a recent course, and her knowledge of Carl's kinaesthetic learning style, Surinder plans a variety of activities to enable him to develop the motor skills and motor memory which will enable him to write his name independently.

The activities include participation in a circuit of gross motor activities to improve shoulder and arm strength and movement before school in the morning; the routine includes rhythmic gymnastics, throwing and jumping skills. In addition he finger-paints his name on large sheets of paper, traces his name in different textures, e.g. rice, sand, fabrics, and rolls modelling clay into sausage shapes and moulds these into the letters in his name. He graduates to using different types of pens including a glitter pen to write his name.

Carl is highly motivated by these activities and is keen to try some of them at home.

Carl needs to develop gross and fine motor skills in order to be able to write. Handwriting activities can become tedious and repetitive over time. Surinder has devised a variety of stimulating and challenging activities to encourage Carl to develop the muscle strength and control he needs in order to be able to write.

Provision to be put in place

Interventions may take the form of one-to-one teaching programmes, for example, a finely structured, multi-sensory reading and spelling programme. Interventions may take other forms: different or additional learning materials or special equipment such as a word-processor with word-predictive software might be included. They might introduce some group, individual or peer support, for example, paired reading or paired spelling which will require extra adult time to plan and to monitor effectiveness.

Reviewing progress

This gives pupils, parents and their teachers an opportunity not just to review the targets but also to reflect on their teaching and learning styles and to make any adjustments to the targets or to the programme. The Code of Practice suggests that pupils should be 'actively involved at an appropriate level in discussions about their Individual Education Plans (IEPs), including target setting and review arrangements' (p. 28).

Case study

Paul has been using multi-sensory teaching to help Jake learn to read and spell a set of NLS Year 1/2 high-frequency words.

He encourages Jake to record his progress on a bar graph. Both he and Jake also look for evidence that Jake has retained and used his knowledge of these words in history and science.

Together they collate the evidence of Jake's progress and Paul helps Jake to present the graph and photocopies of his classwork at the IEP review.

In this case study note how Paul has helped Jake to continuously monitor his progress towards his literacy target and to communicate his progress at the IEP review.

Review arrangements

IEPs should be continually kept under review. The frequency of review will depend on the nature of a pupil's needs and the provision being made to meet those needs. The Code of Practice requires that IEPs are reviewed at least twice a year although many schools do this each term. For pupils with a statement of Special Educational Needs there must be an annual review of the statement.

A review needs to involve all those who have information to contribute; this should include the teacher, TA, parent, pupil and any other relevant agencies and, using the information gathered, adjustments may need to be made to the targets, teaching strategies and programmes in the light of pupil response and changing priorities.

Annual reviews

Higher Level Teaching Assistants have an important and challenging role in helping pupils to prepare for and participate in annual reviews. This challenge increases if the pupil is very young or has communication and/or significant learning difficulties. There has been some interesting and useful work to promote both pupil and parent participation in annual reviews which you may be able to draw on in preparing pupils for annual reviews (Forest, Pearpoint and O'Brien 1996; Hayes 2004).

If the pupil uses alternative forms of communication, you and the pupil could choose symbols to represent the pupil's response to questions about what they like and don't like, feel good at or need to work on, and their reflections on friendships and inclusion in the learning and wider community. Other visual methods such as the 'mosaic approach' can be been used to gain the views of pre-schoolers through building up a picture of their favourite places and people (Clarke and Moss 2001).

As a TA you will have important information of your own to contribute, for example, reporting on how the pupil is responding to individual teaching sessions and by observing whether the pupil is applying skills taught in individual sessions into classroom activities. It is important to maintain your own working records for those pupils that you teach and to make notes about a pupil's response in class to share afterwards with the teacher.

Example of a working record for individual teaching programme

Targets

1. Pupil can segment cvc words orally using a m s t i (90% accuracy × 3 separate occasions – words presented at random)
2. Pupil can blend cvc words orally using a m s t i (90% accuracy × 3 separate occasions – sounds presented at random)
3. Pupil can map grapheme onto phoneme a m s t i using tactile letters (90% accuracy × 3 separate occasions)

Name	Date			
Pupil can segment cvc words orally with a/m/s/t/i				
Pupil can blend cvc words orally a/m/s/t/i				
Pupil can map grapheme onto phoneme using tactile letters				

Key: T= taught P= practised ✓ = correct

A review needs to consider if a pupil is making adequate progress. Paragraph 5:42 on page 52 of the Code of Practice offers states that:

Adequate progress can be defined in a number of ways. It might, for instance, be progress which:

- *closes the attainment gap between the pupil and his/her peers*
- *prevents the attainment gap growing wider*
- *is similar to that of peers starting from the same attainment level but less than that of the majority of their peers*
- *matches or betters the pupil's previous rate of progress*
- *ensures full access to the curriculum*
- *demonstrates an improvement in self-help, social or personal skills*
- *demonstrates improvements in behaviour.*

It is important to note that defining 'adequate progress' is complex because not all pupils will make progress at the same pace and progress is not necessarily a linear process. A pupil may make great gains initially and then progress may level out for a while as the pupil consolidates new learning. A pupil with dyslexic difficulties, for example, is likely to need lots of over-learning of new spelling patterns to ensure retention in long-term memory and even then they may forget to apply their knowledge under stress.

Success and/or exit criteria

Either success criteria or exit criteria are attached to targets. If targets are achieved this may mean either that new targets will need to be set or that an IEP is no longer required. It is important to set small-step achievable targets and ensure that the success criteria are a reasonable indicator that the skill or knowledge is being retained and applied.

Outcomes (to be recorded when IEP is reviewed)

Evaluation of the success of an IEP needs to take into account the strategies employed and the frequency of delivery of the targeted intervention. If targets are not being achieved then the teacher will need to consider all the possible reasons – attendance, teaching strategy, resources, and appropriateness of target. It may be that the target needs breaking down into smaller steps or an alternative target needs to be chosen.

Example of an individual education plan

Individual Education Plan	School Action School Action Plus ✓
Name Andrew	**Address**
DOB	**Telephone**
School	**Parents/Guardians**
Year/Class Y 6	

Focus of IEP		
	Communication	
	Literacy	✓
	Maths	
	Emotional, social, behaviour	
	Physical/sensory	✓

Pupil's strengths
Andrew has a good general knowledge and vocabulary. Participates in whole-class sessions. He is developing decoding strategies for reading and responds well to 1:1 work. He has been successful in using mnemonics for some spelling.

Areas of need
Andrew has specific learning difficulties affecting the development of literacy skills, in particular, planning and writing skills.
He has poor fine motor skills manifested in slow and often illegible handwriting and in tasks requiring cutting and sticking skills.
Andrew feels anxious about his difficulties, particularly writing in the light of the National Curriculum tests in May. His self-esteem is beginning to suffer.

Other agencies/professionals involved
Specialist support teacher for specific learning difficulties.
Support teacher for physical difficulties.

Baseline information
British Picture Vocabulary Scales (2) scored on 92nd percentile, with an age-equivalent score of 13.10.

Neale Analysis of Reading Ability (2)
Reading Accuracy age: 8:07
Reading Comprehension age: 9:01
Reading Rate: 11:08
Vernon Spelling: 7: 05
Writing speed: 8 words a minute

Programme for Andrew_____ from _____ to _____

Completed by _____ Role _____

Targets (including success criteria)
Andrew will be able to:
1. read multi-syllabic words in text (success criterion: 90% accuracy in three consecutive miscue analyses during 6-week block)
2. read with expression, taking account of punctuation, using reading books levelled at 8:05–9:00 (success criterion: miscue shows Andrew is reading more slowly and carefully with attention to accuracy and meaning)
3. split multi-syllabic words up and encode each syllable, achieving 70% success in spelling tests and in supported work
4. use mind-mapping software to plan writing tasks (success criterion: English writing tasks will show improvement in sequencing and organisation of ideas, and use of paragraphs).

Teaching strategies and materials (additional to and different from the differentiated curriculum)
Use of portable word-processor for recording in class
TA support in class for writing tasks
Structured reading and spelling programme to develop awareness and use of syllables
Use of special scissors
Cutting-skills programme at home
Touch-typing programme at ICT club
National Curriculum test access arrangements: reader for all subjects and scribe for science. Investigate additional time.

Arrangements
● 1:1 TA 3 × 20 mins session weekly reading and spelling programme
● assistance with scribing from TA in English and science.

Parental views
Very keen to support Andrew at home:
● will read with him at least four times a week
● practise spellings using multi-sensory methods (explained)
● encourage Andrew to work through cutting exercises

Pupil's views [these may be transcribed or attached]
I am worried about the SATs because of all the reading and writing but I may get a reader and also a scribe for science.
I am looking forward to using a portable word-processor and I like the mind-mapping ideas as I think better in pictures and diagrams.

Review of progress against targets and additional information

Signed

Review date

The IEP format above is only one example of a variety of different formats. Most schools use word-processed forms and many use specific support packages. The format itself is not important if all the criteria in the Code of Practice are addressed and the IEP is a working document recording the process.

> ### PRACTICAL TASK
>
> Look at an IEP for a pupil at School Action Plus.
>
> Identify which agencies are involved and how they contribute to the IEP (advising, teaching, monitoring).
>
> What are the current IEP targets and how do these relate to areas of need and baseline information?
>
> What arrangements are in place to support the IEP?
>
> What teaching strategies and materials are suggested?
>
> What evidence is there of (a) pupil and (b) parent involvement in target-setting implementation and monitoring?

Summary

1. An IEP is an assessment, planning, teaching and reviewing tool setting out the knowledge and skills which will be taught through additional or different activities from those provided for all pupils through the differentiated curriculum and Wave Two provisions.

2. An effective IEP contains SMART targets which are ideally written in collaboration with the pupil and parent, and is continually kept under review.

References

Byers, R. and Rose, R. (2004) *Planning the Curriculum for Pupils with Special Educational Needs*. London: David Fulton.

Clarke A. and Moss, P. (2001) *Listening to Young Children: A Mosaic Approach*. London: NCB.

Department for Education and Skills (2001a) *Special Educational Needs: Code of Practice*. London: DfES.

Department for Education and Skills (2001b) *SEN Toolkit*. London: DfES.

Department for Education and Skills (2002) *Including all Children in the Literacy Hour and Daily Mathematics Lesson*. London: DfES.

Department for Education and Skills (2004) *Removing Barriers to Achievement: The Government's Strategy for SEN*. London: DfES.

Forest, M., Pearpoint, J. and O'Brien, J. (1996) MAPS: Educators, parents, young people and their friends planning together. *Educational Psychology in Practice*, 11 (4), 35–40.

Hayes, J. (2004) Visual annual reviews: how to include pupils with learning difficulties in their educational reviews. *Support for Learning*, 19 (4), 175–180.

Ofsted (1997) *The SEN Code of Practice: two years on*. London: HMSO.

Shotton, G. (2003) *Pupil Friendly Education Plans*. Bristol: Lucky Duck.

Tilstone, C., Lacey, P., Porter, J. and Robertson, C. (2000) *Pupils with Learning Difficulties in Mainstream Schools*. London: David Fulton.

4. Planning for inclusion

Introduction

Any class will contain pupils from different cultures, ethnic groups, languages, religions and socio-economic backgrounds. In addition to these differences a class will contain pupils with a range of needs, abilities, skills, talents, experiences and motivations. A school which values pupils as individual members belonging to a learning community will view any disability as an individual difference rather than as a problem.

The process by which we manage the different learning needs of pupils is called *differentiation*. Differentiation was officially recognised in the National Curriculum through the Education Reform Act of 1988. This Act legislated for every pupil's entitlement to a curriculum which is broad, balanced, relevant and 'subtly' differentiated. The National Curriculum Council defined differentiation as a 'process by which curriculum objectives, teaching methods, assessment methods, resources and learning activities are planned to cater for the needs of individual pupils' (NCC 1991).

In this chapter we will consider the ways in which you as a professional TA can plan with teachers to ensure that all pupils can make progress in their learning. Lack of time for TAs and teachers to plan together has been identified by teachers, TAs and head teachers as a major difficulty. Although professional TAs are not entitled to planning, preparation and assessment (PPA) time, there are obvious benefits in releasing TAs to work with teachers and some schools are working towards providing some joint planning time:

> *sharing out planning between groups of colleagues and involving teaching assistants where appropriate can reduce workload, save time and stimulate discussion. Staff with specific expertise can also bring their specialist knowledge to the process.* (DfES 2004, p. 20)

Your attitude and expectations can make a positive difference to pupils' learning experiences. Showing an interest in individuals' particular needs, abilities and interests and including them in class curriculum activities can make a significant impact on their self-esteem and learning progress.

By observing pupils, their interactions with each other and their response to tasks your insights can support the teacher in curriculum planning and assessment.

This chapter will examine how you can ensure that pupils do make progress through setting appropriate learning objectives that relate to the curriculum and to their own personal targets identified on their Individual Education Plans.

1.1   They have high expectations of all pupils; respect their social, cultural, linguistic, religious and ethnic backgrounds; and are committed to raising their educational achievement.

2.2   They are familiar with the school curriculum, the age-related expectations of pupils...

2.3   They understand the aims, content, teaching strategies and intended outcomes for the lessons...

3.1.1 They contribute effectively to teachers' planning and preparation of lessons.

3.1.3 They contribute effectively to the selection and preparation of teaching resources...

3.3.1 ... they interest and motivate pupils, and advance their learning.

3.3.3 They promote and support the inclusion of all pupils in the learning activities...

3.3.5 ...working with individuals ... small groups ... whole classes...

CHAPTER OBJECTIVES

By the end of this chapter you should be able to identify how you, in association with the teacher, can contribute to the raising of individual achievement through:

- understanding pupil differences
- helping to set suitable learning challenges
- responding to pupils' diverse learning needs
- overcoming potential barriers to learning and assessment for individuals and groups of pupils.

(National Curriculum Inclusion Statement (1999)

Understanding pupil differences

While teachers may plan a lesson for a whole-class group, they cannot assume that everyone will find it challenging and enjoyable. This is because a whole-class group contains a selection of smaller groups and a collection of individuals with:

- **common needs:** all learners have some learning needs that are common
- **exceptional needs:** identified by the needs shared by a group of learners
- **individual needs:** unique to the person.

Norwich (1996, p. 103)

For example, a pupil with dyslexia has:

common needs – (to be respected as an independent learner and a communicator, and to belong to a classroom community)

exceptional needs – (for the teacher to understand the learning styles and access strategies that can support pupils with dyslexia)

individual needs – (for the teacher to identify and understand the differences that make a pupil unique – no two dyslexics have exactly the same pattern of strengths and weaknesses).

PRACTICAL TASK

Think of a class you support and write down the different needs pupils have under the headings below:

COMMON NEEDS	EXCEPTIONAL NEEDS	INDIVIDUAL NEEDS
e.g. safety	e.g. learning style	e.g. regular
respect	support for reading	physiotherapy
belonging		

How do you find out about the particular needs and characteristics of the pupils you support?

Discuss with the class teacher to what extent medium- and short-term planning already takes into consideration the range of needs in the class.

How could the planning be developed further to meet the needs of everyone in the class? (For example, by meeting the needs of a pupil with cerebral palsy who learns best from sensory experiences, games and pictorial worksheets, you make the lesson more interesting and accessible to everyone.)

Setting suitable learning challenges

Not all pupils in a class will be working towards the same learning objectives. It is important to match learning objectives to a pupil's cognitive abilities. This means identifying the things which pupils are good at and those which present them with difficulties and trying to plan activities which build on their strengths. For example, if a pupil is good at drawing but finds difficulties with writing, you might consider ways in which they can produce a picture to demonstrate understanding and then write a caption for this in order to improve their confidence in writing. This will, of course, depend upon the teacher's plans for the activity. If the purpose of the task is to demonstrate understanding, a picture may well be suitable for showing this. If, of course, the activity is about improving handwriting then a picture would not be appropriate.

For some pupils with cognitive delay, it may be necessary to 'track back' to earlier objectives, for example, within the National Literacy Strategy and National Numeracy Strategy.

Case study

Liam is a Year 5 pupil who has a statement of special educational needs relating to difficulties with understanding and using language. This is affecting his development of literacy, numeracy and social skills. In today's lesson Liam's class are working on story writing.

Narinder, the TA in his class, has observed Liam's difficulty in writing sentences unaided. She refers to his IEP and notices that he has a target to write and punctuate simple sentences. She discusses with the teacher how the lesson can be differentiated for Liam so that he is working on a similar learning objective to the rest of the class and addressing his individual targets. She tracks back through the NLS and identifies an appropriate objective from Year 3 Term 1: Revision and consolidation from Key Stage 1, which is to write in complete sentences, demarcating the end of a sentence with a fullstop and the start of a new one with a capital letter. She designs an interactive storyboard which includes a series of randomly ordered pictures, relating to fishing, which is his hobby. The task is to correctly sequence the pictures, write sentences in the box under each one, producing an illustrated story. Liam is able to work on the same task as his peers and address his individual needs.

In the case study above, we can see how the TA has selected an appropriate learning task based on a number of important considerations. Through her observations of Liam in the classroom she was able to identify a need and act on it. She has referred to Liam's IEP and to the National Literacy Strategy to track back and select an appropriate learning objective. The activity that she has planned meets his interests; is pitched at a level at which he can learn and succeed; and links directly with the focus of work for the class as a whole. It is a skill which he can be encouraged to apply in other areas of the curriculum.

In order to ensure that learning objectives are appropriate for individual pupils you need to be familiar with the school curriculum and age-related expectations. It is also useful to have easy access to the relevant curriculum documents to enable you to plan. For example, in one school all the teachers have a complete set of medium-term plans for the National Literacy and Numeracy strategies covering a span of five years, enabling them to track forwards and backwards.

Pre-tutoring is a strategy which prepares pupils to share the learning objectives of the class. It is particularly useful for pupils with language difficulties because it introduces key vocabulary and concepts prior to the lesson and can enable pupils to access a learning objective. For example, pre-teaching the vocabulary associated with a science or mathematical topic using objects, pictures and games to illustrate abstract terms helps pupils to take an active part in the lesson.

Some units of work will not fit directly with the particular learning objectives (IEP targets) for an individual pupil. In this case work will need to be planned that the pupil (or group of pupils) can do in parallel to the main class topic.

Responding to pupils' diverse learning needs

What many teachers may not have considered is the need to differentiate not just because of different abilities but because pupils learn in different ways. Choice needs to take into account the lesson content, learning styles of pupils, emotional and social development of pupils, physical environment, the teaching resources and the experience and confidence of teacher.

Difficulties in learning often arise from... inflexible teaching styles.
(DfES 2004)

Effective planning draws on the experiences and motivation that pupils bring to their learning. This underpins good teaching, which in turn then builds and extends the knowledge of the pupils. Pupils may have a preferred learning style, but while it is important to accommodate these in our teaching, it is also important to strengthen the weaker sensory channels so that pupils learn to use a wider range of learning strategies.

If children cannot learn the way we teach, we must teach them the way they can learn. (Dyslexia Institute)

As a professional TA you need to consider and adjust your support to take into account:

- the challenge and relevance of the curriculum content
- the different strategies that motivate pupils to learn
- pupils' resilience to coping with ambiguity, difficulties and setbacks
- their ability to work co-operatively with others.

All pupils benefit from access to quiet study areas with minimal distractions. For a pupil with autistic spectrum disorder this access may be an essential requirement.

You will find more information in the chapters on learning styles and multi-sensory teaching.

Overcoming potential barriers to learning

For some pupils with SEN, differentiation may involve accelerating their progress through learning objectives while offering support for accessing the curriculum, for example, enlarged reading materials and worksheets for pupils with visual impairment (although you may find that the access strategies essential for some pupils will also be found desirable by other pupils).

This needs to be considered at school level, for example: ensuring that curriculum choices reflect the diverse experiences of pupils relating to race, culture, gender; ensuring the curriculum reflects disability awareness; ensuring all types of bullying are addressed (including racial and homophobic) so that pupils feel safe, secure and valued.

Teaching styles

At classroom level, teachers need to use a variety of teaching styles that are appropriate to the learner's current level of understanding (Wedell 1995) and to the learning activity. Teaching styles can include didactic, discursive and investigative.

Didactic

This is direct teaching where the teacher is leading from the front, for example, informing, describing, explaining, demonstrating, modelling, coaching, questioning. A lesson which is introducing a new idea or concept may begin with a structured exposition which sets out the learning objective and gives the pupils clear concise information as a basis from which to begin an exploration of a topic. Brisk, brief and varied input is an important criterion for effective expositions.

Modelling and demonstrating are techniques often used to model particular skills, e.g. in shared reading and writing. For example, a teacher might demonstrate how to write a description using the features of descriptive writing identified by the pupils from literature they have analysed. In maths, models give pupils a picture or image to help them understand a concept and sequence the steps to solving the problem. Interactive whiteboards are increasingly used to support whole-class teaching.

If the teaching approach is didactic you will need to negotiate your role with the teacher, as there are a number of ways in which you can help pupils to learn. These can include the following.

- Planned observation of individual pupils' behaviour, level of participation, or recording their responses.
- Formative assessment noting who can and can't apply a taught strategy.
- Focusing attention by sitting alongside a pupil or group of pupils and directing their attention by pointing to pictures, text or artefacts under discussion, and offering verbal and non-verbal encouragement to join in.

- Modelling by demonstrating to pupils how to do something, e.g. how to use scissors, work out a number or spelling strategy, or by taking part in a 'double-act' with the teacher.
- Prompting. This can be verbal, physical or both. Tilstone *et al.* (2000) note the importance of 'close prompting' in developing co-attention, which is where both teacher and pupil engage fully with a task.
- Clarifying, for example, rephrasing instructions for pupils who do not understand, supporting the teacher by drawing attention to pupils who need further support or acknowledgement.
- Overlearning. This means offering lots of opportunities for revision to ensure that new information skills and understanding are stored in the long-term memory. Games and computer software are a good way of ensuring revision does not become boring.
- Operating ICT resources.

Discursive

The teacher engages in interactive dialogue with pupils to understand their own concepts and builds on pupils' own knowledge and skills through challenging, questioning, energising, encouraging, clarifying.

This approach draws on effective questioning techniques to extend and improve the quality of dialogue in the classroom. For example, a teacher may sequence questions from literal or closed questions to higher-order or more open questions, differentiating them appropriately. The teacher may give pupils thinking time or invite them to verbalise their thinking with a talking partner to produce more extended and thoughtful responses both after the question and after the answer.

TAs have an important role in lessons where pupils are being asked to talk about their learning. For instance, pupils may be asked to brainstorm or discuss a point which has to be fed back to the class.

There is often limited time available for this discussion. You can help pupils who have difficulties in articulating their thoughts formulate a response through questioning, modelling or scaffolding answers, e.g. by offering sentence starters and letting the teacher know when pupils are ready to respond.

Investigative

One of the principles for early year's education taken from the curriculum guidance for the Foundation stage states that there should be opportunities for pupils to engage in activities planned by adults and also those that they plan or initiate themselves. This is true for all learners.

Investigative teaching offers pupils the opportunity to carry out open-ended 'hands-on' tasks, for example, exploring the properties of wet and dry sand or using the internet to research a topic. Offering opportunities for investigative learning is important because it is a way of teaching pupils how to develop as independent learners; to move away from adult dependence and to participate in self-motivated activity. Investigative learning also offers pupils the opportunity to make links between different curriculum subjects, e.g. using persuasive writing to highlight the issue of water usage in geography. It also encourages the use of knowledge, skills and understanding in new contexts.

Co-operative group work is a useful way of organising pupils for investigative problem-solving tasks. It enables pupils to learn from each other. They do this by discussing their ideas, learning to negotiate and see things from someone else's point of view and arguing their own point of view.

Working as a TA in this context, you will need to consider how you are going to support the pupils to work as a group. Strategies could include drawing up or reminding them of group interaction rules. As well as focusing on specific task outcomes, evaluation of the learning should include how well they worked as a group measured against the group interaction rules.

The role of the TA may include:

- collecting and preparing resources
- observing how pupils approach the task and recording their responses
- supporting pupils to develop their thinking skills through asking questions that assist rather than direct their thinking, e.g. 'so what does that tell us about...?'
- helping pupils to draw on previous experience to help them solve a new problem, e.g. 'what did you do last time?'
- helping them to anticipate and plan, e.g. 'what are you going to do next?'
- challenging responses, e.g. 'but what about...?'
- praising, e.g. 'I like the way that you...'.

Case study

Peter is a TA working in a Year 2 class who are given the task of sorting pictures of animals and plants using grids from the program 'Clicker 4'. Through the use of questioning, discussion and observation, Peter notes the pupils' response to the task. He observes how Tom is able to recognise the similarities between animals and between plants and differences within these groups and give reasons for his groupings. Sally, on the other hand, while recognising that animals and plants are different, applies 'fur' as the criterion distinguishing animals from other living things. This shows an under-inclusive view of animals. Peter is able to feed back this formative assessment to the teacher to assist the planning of the next lesson, and obtain a clear picture of what support Sally and Tom need to advance their learning. Both pupils have special educational needs. Tom has reading and spelling difficulties but strengths in verbal comprehension and reasoning. Sally can decode text and write neatly but has poor vocabulary and understanding. Planning has to take into account their different learning profiles. Challenging learning objectives need to be set for Tom; alternative methods of recording, e.g. mind-mapping, could help him to demonstrate his knowledge and skills. Sally needs increased opportunities to consolidate and extend her understanding of animals through the use of visual materials, introduction and reinforcement of key vocabulary, effective questioning (including a balance of open and closed questions), and clear recording formats.

PRACTICAL TASK

Using the following format as a guide, identify the range of ways in which learning activities are differentiated in a lesson you teach or support. This audit can be an observation of a whole-class or group activity and can be conducted for a sample of different subjects or lessons. When you have completed your observations, ask the class teacher to take some time to discuss your observations with you. The purpose of this task is to discuss the ways in which planning currently enable pupils to access the curriculum and to identify further opportunities for you to support the class teacher in differentiating to meet the needs of pupils with SEN.

Input   What strategies were used to enable the learners to gain new information, ideas and vocabulary?
Tasks   How were the tasks differentiated?
Resources   What range of resources (human and material) was used?
Support   What methods/people were used to support learning?
Outcomes and response   What range of outcomes came from the activity? What kinds of responses were offered at the end of the activity?
Assessment   How were the types of assessment varied throughout the activity to reflect all styles of learning?

Summary

It is clear that the professional TA has an important role in enabling all pupils to become more independent learners and in helping to raise standards of achievement for all pupils. This is achieved through collaborative planning in which both the teacher and the TA bring their experience and understanding of the pupils and their knowledge of resources and curriculum together. Learners need:

- teachers to build on what they already know, understand and are able to do
- provision of alternative learning activities
- clear and immediate feedback
- to take some responsibility for their own learning.

References

Bearne, E. (ed.) (1996) *Differentiation and Diversity in the Primary School*. London: Routledge.

Byers, R. and Rose, R. (2004) *Planning the Curriculum for Pupils with Special Educational Needs*. London: David Fulton.

Department for Education and Skills (2003) *Speaking, Listening, Learning: Working with Children in Key Stages 1 and 2*. London: DfES.

Department for Education and Skills (2004) *Excellence and Enjoyment: Learning and Teaching in the Primary Years*. London: DfES.

McNamara, S. and Moreton, G. (1997) *Understanding Differentiation: a Teacher's Guide*. London: David Fulton.

National Curriculum Council (1991) *Science and pupils with special educational needs. A workshop pack for Key Stages 1 and 2*. York: NCC.

Norwich, B. (1996) Special needs education for all: Connective specialisation and ideological impurity. *British Journal of Special Education*, 23 (3), 100–103.

O'Brien, T. and Guiney, D. (2001) *Differentiation in Teaching and Learning: Principles and Practice*. London: Continuum.

Tilstone, C., Lacey, P., Porter, J. and Robertson, C. (2000) *Pupils with Learning Difficulties in Mainstream Schools*. London: David Fulton.

Weddell, K. (1995) Making inclusive education ordinary. *British Journal of Special Education*, 22 (3), 100–104.

Website addresses

1. visit **www.nc.uk.net/inclusion.html** for National Curriculum inclusion statement
2. visit **www.standards.dfes.gov.uk/primary** and follow links to literacy and maths.
3. visit **www.teachernet.gov.uk** and type 'differentiation' in to search box on home page.

5. Overcoming barriers to learning

Introduction

In Chapter 3 we considered the ways in which you as a professional TA can plan with teachers to ensure appropriate targets are set for all pupils, including those with SEN. It is important not to assume that just because a pupil has a special educational need that they are not capable of working to the same learning objectives as the rest of the class. Pupils can be capable of working towards the same learning objectives as their peers but have difficulties arising from their particular physical, cognitive, or sensory difference which may prevent them from taking part in the lesson.

> *Schools supported by local education authorities and others should actively seek to remove the barriers to learning and participation that can hinder or exclude pupils with special educational needs.* (DfES 2001a)

There is a growing emphasis on the need to focus less on an individual's difference or impairment and more on access, i.e. how the teaching environment can be adapted to meet the learning needs of everyone:

> *Difficulties in learning often arise from an unsuitable environment- inappropriate groupings of pupils, inflexible teaching styles, or inaccessible curriculum materials – as much as from individual children's physical, sensory or cognitive impairments.* (DfES 2004a)

Access strategies ensure that pupils are not prevented from participating in lessons and from assessment opportunities because of their special needs. The role of the professional TA can be seen as an access strategy (DfES 2002) but there are some important issues to consider in defining your role in supporting pupils to access the curriculum. The aim should be to develop pupils' independence and self-esteem and there are several important factors to consider.

Firstly, we need to ensure that the learning objectives are relevant and appropriate for the pupil who is being supported and that the TA is not being used to help the pupil complete inappropriate work just because it's work that the rest of the class is doing. We need to avoid pupils becoming dependent on TAs, believing that they can only succeed with their support; this undermines a child's self-esteem. It is important that the pupil has opportunities to work on their own or supported by peers. We need to ensure that the TA is not inadvertently acting as a barrier to a pupil's interactions with their peers and it is important that the TA works with other pupils in the class too. Support needs to be discrete. We want to develop pupils' independence and self-esteem through providing them with the learning conditions and resources that they need to succeed.

There are a number of DfES publications that you need to become familiar with as these offer practical advice on how to ensure that curriculum and assessment strategies at school and class level allow all pupils to access the curriculum. The following two documents are a useful starting point:

Including All Children in the Literacy Hour and Daily Mathematics Lesson (DfES 2002)

Excellence and Enjoyment: Learning and Teaching in the Primary Years (DfES 2004b).

This chapter considers how teachers and TAs can plan and incorporate specific access strategies in their teaching to enable pupils to take part in a lesson and demonstrate their knowledge, understanding and skills.

HLTA STANDARDS

1.1   They have high expectations of all pupils; respect their social, cultural, linguistic, religious and ethnic backgrounds; and are committed to raising their educational achievement.

2.1   They have sufficient understanding of their specialist area to support pupils' learning, and are able to acquire further knowledge to contribute effectively and with confidence to the classes in which they are involved.

2.2   They are familiar with the school curriculum, the age-related expectations of pupils, the main teaching methods and the testing/examination frameworks in the subjects and age ranges in which they are involved.

2.4   They know how to use ICT to advance pupils' learning...

2.5   They know the key factors that can affect the way pupils learn.

2.9   They know a range of strategies to establish a purposeful learning environment and to promote good behaviour.

3.1.3   They contribute effectively to the selection and preparation of teaching resources that meet the diversity of pupils' needs and interests.

3.3.1   ...they interest and motivate pupils, and advance their learning.

3.3.3   They promote and support the inclusion of all pupils in the learning activities...

CHAPTER OBJECTIVES

By the end of this chapter you should:

- be aware of the potential barriers to learning that exist for pupils who have particular needs in the areas identified in the Code of Practice – cognition and learning, communication and interaction, sensory and physical, and behavioural, emotional, social difficulties

- have considered access strategies which enable pupils to work both independently and collaboratively

- have considered the range of access arrangements for National Curriculum tests.

The Code of Practice identifies four areas of need but each child is unique and it is important to understand that individual pupils may have needs in one or more areas of communication and interaction, cognition and learning, behaviour, emotional and social development and sensory and/or physical difficulties. In order to help pupils overcome barriers to learning it is important to know about the individual needs and characteristics of the pupils you support and some background knowledge about particular special educational needs.

Understanding barriers to learning

Cognition and learning

There are a number of skills that pupils need to function in the classroom: literacy skills, numeracy skills, organisation, memory and comprehension. Some pupils have great difficulty in these areas and require access strategies that ensure that their difficulties don't prevent them from acquiring, generalising and applying new knowledge and which promote self-confidence and self-esteem. Pupils with moderate learning difficulties in mainstream schools are recognised by the DfES as the largest group with SEN whose needs are often overlooked (DfES 2004a).

Dyslexia is another example of a barrier to learning within the area of cognition and learning. It is a combination of strengths, often in artistic, spatial and creative thinking, and weaknesses which affects the acquisition of reading, spelling and writing skills and sometimes number and calculation. Learners with dyslexia may also have additional difficulties such as short-term memory, organisation, sequencing, slow processing and motor co-ordination. It is a hidden disability and because literacy skills are part of everyday classroom life, can have a negative effect on pupil self-esteem.

Communication and interaction

Learning is a social process and learners can develop greater knowledge and skills when working with others than they can on their own. There is therefore an increasing appreciation and promotion of the use of paired and group work. Being a member of a class community requires the ability to listen, to understand, speak clearly, respond appropriately, express thoughts coherently, play and work co-operatively and empathise. Learning in a social context presents challenges for pupils with problems in the area of communication and interaction. The range of difficulties is wide and includes pupils with speech and language difficulties; specific learning difficulties such as dyslexia and dyspraxia; hearing impairment; those who are on the autistic spectrum; and those with moderate, severe or profound learning difficulties.

Overcoming speech, language and communication barriers to learning is recognised as 'crucial to enabling children to access the whole curriculum' (DfES 2004a).

Behaviour, emotional and social development

There are a range of social and emotional skills that pupils need in order to become confident, motivated and independent learners. These are summarised in *Excellence and Enjoyment: Social and Emotional Aspects of Learning* (DfES 2005) as self-awareness, managing feelings, social skills, empathy and motivation. These five aspects of affective learning are taken from the work of Daniel Goleman (1995), who promoted and popularised the concept of 'emotional intelligence'. He asserted that emotional intelligence was more important than cognitive abilities in predicting academic success.

It is recognised that for some children lack of motivation, fear of failure, difficulties in recognising and managing feelings and handling relationships can create significant emotional and social barriers to learning. It is important to realise too that children with learning difficulties can suffer from low self-esteem in an educational context.

Children can demonstrate a range of emotional, social and behavioural responses to difficulties arising from medical, mental or environmental causes or a combination of these factors. Difficulties in this area can be temporary; for example, as a child adjusts to loss of a significant person in their lives, or they can be more persistent over time.

Some pupils have more complex needs arising, for example, from attention deficit hyperactivity disorder and autistic spectrum disorder.

Pupils express their emotional and social needs in different ways. Some can be withdrawn, isolated and lack concentration while others can be challenging, hyperactive and disruptive.

Sensory and physical needs

There are a wide range of sensory, multi-sensory and physical difficulties which pose potential barriers to learning. Sensory difficulties can extend from profound and permanent deafness or visual impairment through to lesser levels of loss, which may be only temporary. Physical difficulties can arise from physical, neurological or metabolic causes that only require appropriate access to educational facilities and needs, while some pupils will have more complex learning and social needs.

A few children will have multi-sensory difficulties, some with associated physical difficulties. For children with the most complex physical needs and the most severe sensory losses, access to specialist teaching and equipment will be needed.

PRACTICAL TASK

Think about the pupils in a class that you support.

What actual or potential barriers to learning exist?

Try to categorise them in the table below.

Which seem to be the most commonly presenting difficulty in the class?

Which are the most difficult to cater for and why?

How do you work with the class teacher to overcome them?

Communication and interaction	Cognition and learning
Behaviour, social and emotional	Physical and sensory

Overcoming barriers to learning

Cognition and learning

Your role as a TA in this key area of SEN is to enable pupils to:

- develop their understanding
- store and retrieve information (memory)
- overcome difficulties in reading, writing and numeracy.

It is important that you are clear about what the learning intention is and not just what the pupils have to do, and that you promote independence as much as possible.

There are a variety of ways in which you can help pupils to access the curriculum. A few strategies are offered here but the needs of individual pupils and the context in which you are working will prompt you to develop a range of creative ways to help pupils learn. You may find the information in Chapters 6 and 7 helpful.

Understanding

- Use the pre-teaching strategy to introduce new vocabulary and concepts (see Chapter 3).
- Use gesture, visual cues or help pupils to read and interpret instructions correctly.
- Play devil's advocate by raising questions or problems or pretending not to understand so the teacher can go through the sequence of instructions.
- Check for understanding by asking the pupil to explain what they have to do.
- Make abstract concepts more concrete by using real objects, signs and symbols, photographs, number lines and threaded beads and computer animations.
- Scaffold tasks by providing cloze procedure, writing frames, multiple choice formats.

Memory

- Remind pupils of teaching points. Use pictures and artefacts where possible.
- Provide prompt cards using objects, pictures, signs or key words where there are a sequence of steps to follow in a task.
- Use a dictaphone to record instructions which pupil can play back.
- Model and encourage pupils to use sticky notes, jottings, individual whiteboards to record key words as an *aide-mémoire*.

Literacy difficulties

- Read questions to the pupil.
- Encourage peer support and interaction.
- Cue the pupil in to reading task by highlighting or pointing out new vocabulary.
- Alternatives to writing include: mind-mapping, oral presentation, sorting and ordering symbol cards, predictive or voice-operated word-processing software, labelling diagrams, dictation to a helper, making 2D or 3D displays.

Case study

Sam is a Year 5 pupil who is verbally bright (his understanding of vocabulary as measured by the British Picture Vocabulary Scale is 13:10 at age 10:00). He has a wide general knowledge and a particular skill in demonstrating magic tricks which he has performed in front of the whole school. He does, however, have significant problems with personal organisation, reading and writing and is beginning to develop avoidance tactics in lessons where these skills are required.

His TA, Jane, and teacher have put in place a number of access strategies for Sam but which are available to everyone. Displays around the room give prompts and reminders about what to do, where to find things, and lists of useful words which are colour-coded and organised so children can find words easily. Everyone has word lists, prompts and personal targets on their tables. A visual timetable is displayed to help everyone to anticipate and plan what they need for different activities and homework tasks.

Careful consideration has been given to where to seat Sam and which groups to place him in so that he has opportunities to work with peers who will benefit from his ideas and knowledge and who can support his literacy needs, e.g. by reading instructions.

Opportunities are made available to enable Sam to access information in a variety of different ways, e.g. pictures, flow charts, drama, and through the use of computer software.

Alternative ways of recording ideas enable Sam to demonstrate his knowledge, skills and understanding. Sometimes Sam dictates his work to the TA. It is important that he has opportunities to do this now as he is likely to need this access arrangement in the National Curriculum tests next year. In group or paired activities, a fluent writer often does the scribing. Sam enjoys giving oral presentations and also likes to record his ideas using mind-mapping and posters. Sam is learning to touch type and to use talking word processing software. As he becomes more competent in this skill, it is likely to be his preferred means of recording in the future.

In this case study the TA and the teacher have worked together to adapt the classroom and curriculum arrangements to enable Sam to become an independent learner. Sam's individual needs have actually been the catalyst in the development of an inclusive classroom which is not just not just meeting Sam's needs but benefiting everyone. Note also how access planning for Sam is taking into consideration his long-term needs, for example, ensuring that word-processing skills are sufficiently developed to enable him to rely on this method of recording as normal practice in the future.

Communication and interaction

As a professional TA you may implement specific programmes to improve speech articulation, understanding and expressive language, or the social uses of language (pragmatics), under the guidance of a speech and language therapist. You may help pupils to use augmentative and alternative methods of communication such as Makaton sign language.

As a TA you can support pupils' access to learning by enabling them to participate in whole-class and group activities, using their developing skills or alternative methods of communication.

Examples include:

- using visual instructions, e.g. key words or symbols to accompany speech
- using short, precise sentences where the important information is given at the beginning
- helping a pupil to rehearse verbal contribution to group or class discussion
- offering forced alternatives, 'was it night or day?'
- creating posters with pupils to present key vocabulary which is then available as a reference.

Case study

Suzanne is a TA in a unit for pupils with moderate learning difficulties within a primary school. She attends a series of Makaton training workshops because some of the pupils coming into the unit are using Makaton sign language. To ensure that this system of communication can be shared by other members of the school community she teaches Makaton signs to the whole school at Friday assemblies. Suzanne attends singing practice and uses Makaton as a visual support to include all pupils, including those with EAL and those who cannot see or read the words on the OHP.

Makaton sign language is used by the head teacher as she greets the whole school at assembly and has been so successful that a Makaton club has been formed which is open to all pupils.

Again, note how in endeavouring to meet the individual needs of pupils with communication difficulties, Suzanne has been instrumental in ensuring that the whole-school curriculum reflects disability awareness, and in promoting the development of an inclusive school community.

Behaviour, emotional, social development

There are a number of strategies that you can fairly easily implement which benefit all children, but which are particularly important for the inclusion of children with emotional, social and behavioural barriers to learning.

- The first and most important way is by giving pupils recognition and acceptance. This can be achieved by showing an interest in their hobbies, using their interests in teaching activities and by offering unobtrusive assistance in the classroom.
- For pupils who for a variety of reasons do not receive the attention and nurturing they need, meeting and greeting them in the morning can get the day off to a positive start.
- Sitting alongside a pupil with concentration difficulties can help them settle and get involved in the lesson.
- Focusing the attention of inattentive pupils on the teacher by directing them to look and answer questions.
- Providing positive feedback to encourage learning and build self-esteem. It is important to set short-term, easily achievable goals and gradually increase expectations to avoid increasing stress.
- Providing take-up time to enable the pupil to engage with a task is important.
- The language that you use rather than any specific programmes or methods can help to create a secure learning environment.

Hughes and Vass (2001) describe the importance of using the language of possibility, the language of hope and the language of success. They give an example of how you could respond to 'I always get X wrong' with 'Yes, you did get it a bit mixed up but let's see which bit is causing you problems.'

These approaches, along with structured curriculum activities to develop social and emotional competencies, for example, the DfES (2005) Social and Emotional Aspects of Learning (SEAL) programme and circle time, will meet most pupils' emotional and social needs.

Those pupils with more complex needs will require additional support. As a professional TA you may find yourself working with Behaviour Support Services, educational psychologists, and staff from child and adolescent mental health services. You may be able to provide useful information and observations about a child's behaviour which can help everyone in identifying the antecedents and triggers for unwanted behaviours.

An important role for the professional TA can be in supporting pupils to use strategies and arrangements identified on their IEPs either at School Action or at School Action Plus. You may be asked to help implement specialised behavioural and cognitive approaches. Behavioural approaches require consistent implementation of planned strategies. It will be important to notice, affirm and reinforce good behaviour as often as possible using descriptive praise and maybe stickers or tokens. These can be traded for a reward that the pupil has chosen. For example, a reward might be a five-minute game of football in the playground or a table game to be played with a chosen friend.

Cognitive approaches include helping a child to recognise problems and develop problem-solving approaches to managing tricky situations. The child may need help to access and apply taught strategies, for example, using anger-management techniques such as a quiet place or time out. They will also need help in reflecting on their behaviour, making reparation if necessary and rebuilding self-esteem after loss of control.

Professional TAs who have trained in behaviour management may be asked to implement self-esteem programmes or organise social skills or anger management groups but it is important to have been trained to use such materials.

Case study

Lucy is a TA in a Year 1 class and has been supporting James, a pupil who can display aggressive behaviour when playing with other children in unstructured situations. James has been attending a special school for one day a week for observation and teaching. His parents have attended a parents' group at the school.

Lucy attends a meeting with James' parents and staff from the local special school to review his progress and to revise his IEP in the light of the work he has been doing. She discusses the triggers for his aggressive behaviour and the strategies which are helping James to play more successfully with other children. Lucy learns that James' poor communication skills are preventing him from interacting with other children appropriately, causing him to push and hit children.

Lucy plans with the SENCo and class teacher to implement the strategies that are proving effective in the special school setting in managing James' behaviour. She plans to use stories and role play to model appropriate ways of demonstrating how to join in activities. She will also help James practise these skills in games with a group of children from his class. Appropriate behaviour will be rewarded with descriptive praise, e.g. ' Good – I like the way you asked if you could play.'

Furthermore she will liaise with James' parents to share his achievements with them using a home–school diary and they will maintain a sticker chart to reward good behaviour in school. They in their turn will keep Lucy informed of progress towards home targets to establish bedtime and meal routines, thereby raising James' and his parents' self-esteem.

In this case study Lucy has been able to draw on the work James and his parents have been doing in a special school setting. After discussion with the SENCo and other professionals she has been able to implement a specific programme to address James' difficulties in his own school.

The programme is teaching James the skills he needs to join in and integrate successfully with his peers as well as managing his behaviour through the use of descriptive praise and stickers. Crucially, the parents are actively involved in the programme through the home–school diary and donating the stickers. This is important for their self-esteem too.

Lucy has enabled James to continue developing the social skills he needs to become a respected and valued member of his classroom community, thereby improving his self-esteem.

Sensory and physical needs

Pupils with sensory and physical difficulties need a physical environment which has been designed and organised to help them move around the school and access learning support and resources easily, safely and as independently as possible. The kinds of arrangements that may be needed are detailed in the Special Needs Code of Practice, p. 88, and include:

- appropriate furniture to enable pupils to participate with their peers in all parts of the curriculum
- good lighting
- alternative or augmentative forms of communication
- appropriate acoustics and access to amplification systems
- access to low-vision aids
- tactile and kinaesthetic materials
- access to specialist support, e.g. physiotherapists.

As Tilstone *et al.* (2000) note, it is not simply a matter of ensuring wheelchair access and appropriate toileting facilities.

A pupil who needs a Rollator to move around the school has needs which are the same as any other pupil in the school, for example, to participate fully in school and class activities and to be able to work and to play with other pupils.

Case study

Patrick is 10 years old. He has Duchenne muscular dystrophy. His muscle strength is deteriorating and he can no longer bear his weight effectively. This means that he needs to use a wheelchair to access playtimes and school trips. Matt, a TA, provides discreet additional staff supervision on the playground. He has instructed Patrick and his friends on the safety aspects of using a wheelchair on the playground. The friends are allowed to push him and have organised a buddy system during playtimes. There is also a bench where Patrick can sit safely and communicate at the same eye level with his friends.

As Patrick is eventually going to use an electric-powered wheelchair, Matt has been in touch with the Royal Society for the Prevention of Accidents to organise a wheelchair proficiency programme for Patrick which will run parallel to the cycling proficiency scheme for pupils in Year 6.

Patrick uses a special chair on a wheeled base in the classroom. This is height-adjustable, enabling him to work alongside his peers. Matt has done moving and handling training to support him in assisting Patrick to move safely from chair to wheelchair or toilet. Patrick uses his standing frame (as prescribed by the physiotherapist) during art and DT when the other children are standing up. Some of Patrick's exercises and routines are included in warm-ups during PE lessons. Where the class activities are not appropriate, Patrick acts as referee or scorekeeper.

Patrick has a quiet voice and speaks very slowly. The teacher uses a strategy, 'think, pair, share' (30 seconds to think, 1 minute to share with a partner) outlined in the Primary Strategy for encouraging classroom talk. This strategy gives everyone, including Patrick, time to think and to formulate a response. Matt supports Patrick and his talking partner by starting off the discussion, and scribing ideas on a whiteboard, ensuring that he is able to contribute to class discussion.

Although Patrick learnt keyboard skills during Key Stage 1, in anticipation that his upper body strength would weaken, he quickly tires. Matt has found the software program 'Clicker 4' to be an effective way of enabling Patrick to write more easily and independently. Matt produces grids which enable Patrick to input keywords and phrases into his writing. Sometimes Matt will scribe for him.

Matt has built up a trusting relationship with Patrick's parents and they work together to support Patrick's emotional needs as he becomes more aware of his condition and its impact on his life.

Matt is working closely with Patrick, his parents, the class teacher and outside agencies to plan and manage Patrick's inclusion within the class. The focus is on helping Patrick to be as independent as possible, while managing a deteriorating medical condition. Note the emphasis on including Patrick in the social life of the school and in enabling him to access the curriculum, and not on Patrick's physical disability.

Access arrangements for National Curriculum tests

These are based on a pupil's history of need and on what is normal classroom practice. The purpose of access arrangements is to remove any disadvantage arising from a pupil's disability without compromising the assessment of their skills, knowledge or understanding. There are a range of access strategies to enable pupils with visual impairment, hearing impairment, physical difficulties, medical problems and specific learning difficulties to access the tests. Some of the arrangements are at the school's discretion and some have to be applied for. As a professional TA you may be asked to be a prompter, reader or an amanuensis (scribe), to supervise rest breaks and, if you have the appropriate skills, to sign or communicate for a pupil with hearing impairment. There are strict regulations governing how these roles are performed and training should be provided. Information about access arrangements is available from the QCA annually.

PRACTICAL TASK

- Identify a pupil with a statement of special educational need and ask if you can see a copy of their statement and their current IEP.

- What are the main objectives (long-term aims) of the statement?

- What facilities, equipment, staffing arrangements and curriculum are specified?

- What IEP objectives have been identified?

- Does the IEP specify particular strategies or teaching styles which will enable the pupil to access the curriculum and, if appropriate, National Curriculum tests?

- Ask if the teacher will spend some time with you to look at how the teacher annotates short- and/or medium-term planning to include access arrangements in support of this pupil's learning and social inclusion. You will find Section 4 of *Including All Children in the Literacy Hour and Daily Mathematics Lesson* (DfES 2002) helpful.

Summary

Teachers and professional TAs need to work in partnership to respond to pupils' diverse needs. This can be achieved through careful school and curriculum planning which anticipates potential barriers to learning and the creative use of access strategies to overcome any difficulties. Professional TAs offer discreet support so that pupils can work independently, interact with their peer group and participate fully in school life.

References

Department for Education and Skills (2001a) *Special Educational Needs: Code of Practice*. London: DfES.

Department for Education and Skills (2001b) *Guidance to Support Pupils with Specific Needs in the Daily Mathematics Lesson*. London: DfES.

Department for Education and Skills (2001c) *Inclusive Schooling: Children with Special Educational Needs*. London: DfES.

Department for Education and Skills (2002) *Including All Children in the Literacy Hour and Daily Mathematics Lesson*. London: DfES.

Department for Education and Skills (2004a) *Removing Barriers to Achievement: The Government's Strategy for SEN*. London: DfES.

Department for Education and Skills (2004b) *Excellence and Enjoyment: Learning and Teaching in the Primary Years*. London: DfES.

Department for Education and Skills (2005) *Excellence and Enjoyment: Social and Emotional Aspects of Learning*. London: DfES.

Goleman, D. (1995) *Emotional Intelligence: Why it Can Matter More Than IQ*. New York: Bantam.

Gross, J. (1993) *Special Educational Needs in the Primary School: a Practical Guide*. Buckingham: Open University Press.

Hughes, M. and Vass, A. (2001) *Strategies for Closing the Learning Gap*. Stafford: Network Educational Press.

Long, R. and Fogell, J. (1999) *Supporting Pupils with Emotional Difficulties: Creating a Caring Environment for All*. London: David Fulton.

Qualifications and Curriculum Authority. *Years 3-6: Assessment and Reporting Arrangements*. Norwich: QCA Publications. Available at www.qca.org.uk

Tilstone, C., Lacey, P., Porter, J. and Robertson, C. (2000) *Pupils with Learning Difficulties in Mainstream Schools*. London: David Fulton.

6. Multi-sensory learning and teaching

Introduction

There is very little evidence as yet to suggest that teaching to different learning styles actually improves pupils' achievement (Stahl 1999, p. 29). If we reflect, however, on the lessons we remember enjoying the most at school, they are likely to be lessons that grabbed our attention through stimulating one or more of our senses.

This chapter investigates how we can use our understanding of learning styles and multiple intelligences to make learning more memorable through multi-sensory teaching strategies.

HLTA STANDARDS

1.1 They have high expectations of all pupils; respect their social, cultural, linguistic, religious and ethnic backgrounds; and are committed to raising their educational achievement.

2.4 They know how to use ICT to advance pupils' learning...

2.5 They know the key factors that can affect the way pupils learn.

2.9 They know a range of strategies to establish a purposeful learning environment and to promote good behaviour.

3.1.3 They contribute effectively to the selection and preparation of teaching resources that meet the diversity of pupils' needs and interests.

3.3.1 Using clearly structured teaching and learning activities, they interest and motivate pupils, and advance their learning.

3.3.3 They promote and support the inclusion of all pupils in the learning activities...

CHAPTER OBJECTIVES

By the end of this chapter you should:

● appreciate the conditions required for learning to take place and how these might be achieved

● have an understanding of multiple intelligences and their significance for pupils and teachers

● understand the benefits of multi-sensory teaching in enabling pupils to receive, store and retrieve information using the different sensory channels

▶

- understand the difficulties pupils may experience in accessing, storing and retrieving information using the different sensory channels

- have considered how to adapt your teaching to activate pupils' sensory channels (pathways)

- have considered how to raise pupils' awareness of how to use their sensory channels, i.e. learning how to learn in order to develop independence.

Multiple intelligences

People learn best when they have frequent opportunities to learn in their preferred style. (Hughes 2002)

Gardner (1983) suggested that multiple intelligences play an important part in assisting all children to recognise their learning preferences, and teachers in valuing their particular strengths and talents. He identified seven key intelligences prior to adding 'naturalist' and 'existentialist' at a later date.

Linguistic *Activities*: Sensory/exaggerated storytelling Listening to story tapes Labelling areas/objects in the classroom	● Enjoys words/verbal communication ● Good with language ● Aware of patterns ● Reads, writes and spells easily ● Good memory for detail
Logical mathematical intelligence *Activities:* Practise estimating things like size, quantity, weight, etc. Use lists of instructions to follow Use of charts and graphs to gather information	● Good at manipulating numbers ● Picks out patterns and relationships ● Deals in abstract symbols ● Enjoys problem-solving and applying logic ● Values precision and order
Visual spatial intelligence *Activities:* Develop visual symbols for recording information Use of mind maps Use of visual images in films/videos Use of visual images in classroom displays Learning opportunities by watching others	● Good at visualising images in 3D ● Can rotate and manipulate mental images ● May think in pictures ● Can predict the effects of movement (self or object) ● Able to design/construct 3D images ● Facility with diagrams ● Likes information that is presented visually photos, symbols, etc.
Bodily kinaesthetic intelligence *Activities:* Use of role play/drama Opportunities to use physical movements in learning	● Very good control of body ● Enjoys physical movement ● Well developed sense of touch ● Likes to participate ● May fidget and finds it difficult to sit still

Provide with appropriate items to manipulate when learning Practical activities such as art/craft, movement play, pottery etc. Opportunities for movement in a lesson	● Likes to manipulate objects
Musical intelligence *Activities:* Use of music to indicate activities/events Use of songs in learning Turn important information into songs Have a selection of favourite music for the pupil Choose music to reflect different moods Choose music to indicate types of work	● Highly developed musical intelligence may be apparent at a very young age ● Sensitive to pitch, tone and rhythm ● Enjoys listening to music ● Good sound discrimination
Interpersonal intelligence *Activities:* Work with others in small groups Participate in a school council Work with others on problem-solving tasks Provide opportunities to see other pupils and staff, e.g. running a tuck shop Working with younger children within the school Helping others – responsibility Opportunities within the PSHE/citizenship curriculum Relationship play/intensive interaction	● Good understanding or likes being with people ● Sensitive to moods and intentions ● Enjoys communication through a variety of means ● Empathises, able to predict people's reactions ● Enjoys company, sociable
Intrapersonal intelligence *Activities:* Providing pupils with time for self-reflection Teaching about feelings Social stories Review things that went well and why	● Self-motivated ● Well developed sense of identity ● Awareness of own strengths and weaknesses ● Strong sense of values
Naturalist intelligence *Activities:* Learn about the weather Learn about and practise growing things Keep a pet and learn how to look after it Watch nature programmes Collect and work with natural materials within other contexts Learn about marine and wildlife	● Enjoys working in a natural environment ● Has a preference for natural materials ● Is able to remember names of things found in nature ● Understand natural forces and rhythms ● Has a close affinity with animals and nature
Existentialist *Activities:* Provide pupils with opportunities to discuss and debate Give pupils thinking tools and strategies, e.g. philosophy in schools	● Pupils like to ask the big questions: 'why are we here?'

Gardner argued that many educational institutions tend to draw too heavily on logical/mathematical and linguistic intelligences in curriculum planning and that this puts pupils whose strengths lie in other intelligences at a disadvantage. This includes pupils with learning difficulties, who may have particular weaknesses in these areas.

Case study

Kingsley Special School investigated the learning environment, teaching and learning styles to inform the development of a teaching and learning strategy. They found that:

- *teachers taught to their own preferred style*

- *teachers chose books which they wanted to read rather than pupils choosing books which they themselves found interesting*

- *adults gave choices to children and then ignored the choice – 'I know they don't like that'*

- *the entrance to school had little sound or texture to indicate that the pupils have arrived/are leaving – now has distinctive smell, music and a wind chime, they are looking to address textures*

- *classrooms did not always have a defined area for each pupil to 'own'*

- *drinks (water) only available as part of routine of day, not constantly available for children*

- *learning objectives were not always shared with the pupils*

- *sometimes the most difficult concepts were being taught at times of the day when pupils were less likely to be alert (e.g. after swimming)*

- *the school needed to consider the needs of kinaesthetic learners, e.g. those children who need to fiddle or be physically active.*

As a result of actions following their investigation they:

- *established use of a learning environment checklist in all classes*

- *established use of new lesson planning in all classes to include learning styles*

- *trialled new learning style assessments at the start of year*

- *renamed class groups; names were chosen by the school council*

- *involved the school council in reviewing the beginning of the school day and designed more input to ensure positive environment*

- *teachers' performance management targets were linked to increasing independence in learning*

- *learning strategies become part of ongoing professional discussion.*

Memory and learning

There is scientific evidence that indicates that we remember everything we ever experience. We store away every sight, sound, smell and experience that has happened to us since we were born and many from before we were born. The problem for learners is not with storing information; it is with recall. The human brain is able to hold 5–9 items in short-term memory and it can hold information up to 15 seconds. Therefore, there is a real danger that large amounts of information will be forgotten quickly. Reviewing information on a regular basis can significantly improve memory.

For many pupils with learning difficulties this is a complicated issue and many pupils are likely to exhibit some or most of the associated difficulties listed below.

Long reaction time	• Most pupils with learning difficulties need more time to respond to learning. Provide opportunities for learning responses that may be considerably delayed and ensure that all staff are familiar with the ways in which the pupil responds
Low efficiency in processing information	• Small steps in learning including opportunities for revisiting
Failure to learn from past experience	• Provide opportunities in which pupils can be helped to generalise experience in individual, small-group and whole-group situations • Try to ensure that where possible the context for learning relates to real-life experiences rather than closed tasks
Poor attention	• Exploit the beginning of sessions in order to gain the pupil's interest • Use exaggerated teaching techniques including sensory storytelling and creative expression • Reflect the pupil's own behaviour to gain and develop attention – 'intensive interaction' • Provide learning in ways which provide input into all the senses • Remember to connect into their values – use things that push their buttons
Preferences to other stimulus	• Connect with pupils' specific interests • Use pupils' interests to provide a way in and a connection with other forms of learning • Intensive interaction approaches

▶

Inability to examine contents stored in memory	• Use of consistent visual cues pictures/symbols to assist memory • Group information into 'sets' or 'chunks' • Pictures/video of the pupil undertaking the activity • Photograph books of past achievements
Little knowledge about thinking and learning	• Provide opportunities to develop study skills. • Model and encourage rehearsal strategies in learning. • Encourage pupils in developing their potential as independent learners. • Provide sufficient opportunities for choice and decision making throughout the school.

Multi-sensory teaching

Multi-sensory teaching is the simultaneous use of eyes, ears, hands and mouth (and even taste sometimes) to utilise all pathways to the brain when learning. It is appropriate for all learners, whatever their learning style, and is particularly beneficial for learners who experience difficulties in abstract thinking processes which involve working with symbols (e.g. letters and numbers) and ideas.

Sensory channels

Visual channel

> It is believed that babies think in pictures before they develop the ability to think in words, and this visual memory remains strong and vivid. (Mortimore 2003, p. 191)

This is a powerful sensory channel for many learners, including pupils with dyslexia and those on the autistic spectrum. It is important, however, to understand that that it is not the preferred sensory modality for all pupils with dyslexia or autism.

Pupils with a strong visual channel may have some or all of the following cluster of strengths:

- a photographic memory – the ability to describe something in detail
- use of imagery – the ability to think in pictures. Einstein, for example, stated that it was his use of imagery that enabled him to produce the theory of relativity
- ability to scan – the ability to skim through a mass of information to gain an overall impression or understanding or to locate a particular item (e.g. a word or image)

- quick recall of visual images – the ability to quickly assimilate and express an image, for example, the ability to provide police with an accurate witness statement.

On the other hand, pupils with a weak visual channel may:

- have a poor recall of visual images
- confuse visually similar images and words
- be able to visualise the whole but not the parts
- have difficulty reading aloud
- read a word on one line but not on the next
- miss or repeat lines when reading.

Teaching strategies

All learners can benefit from direct teaching which strengthens this sensory channel:

- Activities to improve their visual perception
  - matching
  - spot the difference.
- Activities to improve their visual memory
  - copying pegboard or block patterns
  - Kim's game
  - alphabet arc activities
  - matching pairs games which require pupils to remember the position of different cards.
- There are a number of software programs that target memory training and which include visual memory activities.
- Activities to improve visual motor co-ordination
  - increased opportunities to work with modelling materials, paint, tearing, cutting and pasting and mosaics
  - using jigsaw puzzles of varying difficulties including puzzles pupil has created
  - copying movements, e.g. Simon says.

As a professional TA you can help your pupils utilise their visual channel through:

- ensuring pupils are sitting comfortably with material directly at midline
- visual presentations, e.g. interactive whiteboards, Powerpoint, DVD/CD-ROM, video clips, films
- reinforcing verbal presentations with visual cues, e.g. digital photographs, diagrams, pictures, cartoons, charts, graphs
- when presenting new vocabulary or spellings to learn, encouraging pupils to represent these with their own visual memory hooks

- careful presentation of worksheets/work cards which take into consideration spacing, chunking of information, e.g. using text boxes, background colour, appropriate size of print and choice of font
- changing background colour, font size and colour on computers if appropriate
- provision of text magnifiers and maskers to improve pupil's ability to track print if this helps
- teaching and developing mind-mapping techniques – there are some software programs that help pupils to construct mind maps
- word searches and anagrams
- offering visual ways in which pupils can demonstrate their knowledge and understanding, e.g. posters, writing frames, story boards
- spelling: visual mnemonics e.g. BECAUSE (**B**ig **E**lephants **C**an't **A**lways **U**se **S**mall **E**xits).

Not all pupils are visual learners but all will benefit from being helped to develop this modality.

Auditory channel

This is an important channel to develop because the demand on pupils' listening skills increases as they progress through the educational system. Research has also shown that by the age of 16, skilled readers recall more from written information than visual modes (Wood 1988).

Pupils with a strong auditory modality may:

- achieve rapid, accurate intake of verbal information, e.g. they are able to benefit from lecture-style presentations
- be very focused when listening, e.g. they are able to extract the important information
- listen selectively, e.g. they can ignore outside noises
- have quick recall, e.g. they are able to remember telephone numbers and instructions

This channel should not be confused with the physical ability to hear. A pupil may have perfect hearing but struggle to access, store and retrieve information using this modality. Conversely, a pupil with a hearing impairment may prefer this channel of learning.

Pupils with a weak auditory modality may:

- frequently mishear or misunderstand
- be easily distracted by sound
- have poor recall of orally presented information
- be unable to pronounce multi-syllable words, e.g. 'certificate' may be articulated as 'stifficate'

- have difficulty distinguishing between similar sounds
- be unable to blend sounds together
- confuse names and sounds of letters
- be unable to follow a series of instructions
- have difficulty reciting sequences – days of the week, months of the year or the alphabet
- have difficulty in word-finding, e.g. be able to describe the object that people put up when it is raining but be unable to retrieve the word 'umbrella'.

Teaching strategies

All pupils can benefit from direct teaching which strengthens this sensory channel. The following ideas are by no means an exhaustive list of ideas.

- Activities to improve auditory perception
  - identifying and locating sounds in the environment
  - identifying sounds that are the same or different
  - sound lotto
  - clapping and copying rhythms
  - guessing games – pupil names beginning sound of something s/he can see and class tries to guess the object
  - Chinese whispers.
- Activities to improve auditory memory
  - games that build up a sequence to remember, for example, ' I went on holiday and I packed...'
  - listening comprehensions
  - following a set of oral instructions beginning with one step and increasing to two steps and beyond following instructions to draw a picture or make a model.

As a professional TA you can help your pupils utilise their auditory channel through:

- careful attention to the pupils' learning environment – minimise distractions by sitting pupils away from doors and windows when required to listen
- encouraging eye contact
- keeping sentences short and simple
- stressing key words in sentences with exaggerated intonation
- encouraging pupils to repeat instructions aloud before attempting to carry them out
- encouraging 'internalised talk': 'I will write the title and the date'
- encouraging pupils to seek clarification or repetition of instructions if they haven't understood or remembered an instruction

- leaving time between instructions for pupils to process the information
- checking pupils' understanding as a story is read
- teaching mnemonic strategies to recall spellings or key vocabulary.

Oral kinaesthetic channel

Some pupils are natural verbalisers while others use this learning channel in spite of a limited vocabulary or word-finding difficulties because their visual modality is weaker. Pupils with a strong oral channel respond strongly to words:

> *I've never been able to read very well because of my dyslexia ... I would learn from Jamaican records and street poets. I used to love rhyme and music.*
>
> (Zephaniah 2000)

Pupils strong in this modality may be articulate, have clear speech and be able to recite rhymes/poems. Conversely, pupils with a weak oral channel may mumble or rush their speech and confuse similar sounds, e.g. f/th.

The ability to articulate is an important skill in learning to spell. It can help strengthen sound/symbol correspondence and supports sequential memory. You may be implementing programmes such as 'Cued Articulation' to develop this modality under the direction of a speech and language therapist.

Teaching strategies

- Encourage pupils to feel and see the mouth and tongue movement as sounds or words are spoken.
- Encourage pupils to sub-articulate sounds or words when writing.
- Ensure that pupils repeat words, phrases and sentences for dictation before and during writing.
- Use oral patterns, e.g. Wed-nes-day; sa-id
- use mnemonics. There are some well known mnemonics for irregular words such as BECAUSE: '**B**ig **E**lephants **C**an't **A**lways **U**se **S**mall **E**xits'. The most memorable mnemonics are those that the pupil creates.
- Practise repeating rhymes and poems.
- Use role play and drama.
  Use oral kinaesthetic sensations to overcome letter confusions, e.g.
  'b' – lips together
  'd' – lips apart
  'f' – unvoiced; a puff of air
  'v' – voiced; vibration of teeth on bottom lip.

As a professional TA you can help your pupils utilise their oral kinaesthetic channel through:

- Careful introduction of new words to extend pupils' vocabulary so that they benefit from this modality. Recent research suggests that successful retrieval of new words depends on learning the meaning and phonological pattern, e.g. initial sound and number of syllables (Mortimore 2003, p. 229).

- Encouraging pupils to put information into their own choice of words.
- Enabling them to read text aloud to themselves.
- Allowing them to work with partners to talk through new information and ideas.
- Encouraging them to explain what they have learned to another pupil.
- Preparing oral presentations to the group.
- Encouraging pupils to talk through what they are doing as they do it.
- Articulating ideas before they write.
- Mind-mapping – mind maps can be drawn up without pictures but are more powerful with the inclusion of visual clues.

Tactile kinaesthetic channel

This is another powerful sensory modality for many learners. Younger children and pupils struggling to understand abstract concepts benefit in particular from kinaesthetic teaching. Kinaesthetic learners learn best through touch and movement, for example in role play and practical tasks such as design technology projects and science experiments. They enjoy working in 3D, and may have neat handwriting and have a writing style which flows.

Those whose tactile kinaesthetic modality is weak may have hands which don't do what they should and have difficulty manipulating zips, tying shoe laces and fastening buttons.

Teaching strategies

- Help pupils to relax hand and arm muscles when holding a pen or pencil.
- Using hands to sign helps pupils to learn letter sounds, e.g. Jolly Phonics or cued articulation.
- Finger tracing; see Fernald/SOS technique later in this chapter.
- Use wooden and tactile letters – identify with eyes closed so pupils can feel letters and letter formation.
- Use a variety of writing media: paint, crayon, chalk, glue sticks, etc.
- Write on different textures, e.g. salt, sand, rice, velvet.
- Model letters in modelling clay or make letter/word-shaped biscuits.
- Write in the air.
- Write on outside wall with a 'squeezy' bottle or water pistol.

As a professional TA you can help your pupils utilise their tactile kinaesthetic channel through:

- working with apparatus or concrete situations first to help pupils understand abstract number or mathematical or language concepts
- using role play, hot-seating and freeze-frame helps pupils to understand characterisation and situations in history and English.

PRACTICAL TASK

Reflect on a lesson that you have either taught or observed.

What examples of multi-sensory teaching did you observe?

How did the pupil(s) respond? (Consider attention, motivation, persistence and progression in their learning.)

In what ways could the multi-sensory input have been enhanced further?

You may find the following recording format helpful:

Learning channel	Teacher input	Learner response	Recommendations for future session
Visual modality			
Auditory modality			
Oral kinaesthetic modality			
Tactile kinaesthetic modality			

Case study

Justin is a Year 4 pupil who has been receiving some additional support for his spelling difficulties. He has been using the method 'look, cover, write, check' to learn his weekly spellings taken from the National Literacy Strategy Year 1/2 spelling list.

Chris, the TA, is concerned that although Justin usually achieves good marks in the weekly spelling test, he is unable to transfer this spelling knowledge into his classwork. Drawing on her knowledge of multi-sensory teaching, Chris reflects that Justin's current learning method is relying on visual perception and memory.

Chris has observed that Justin is a very tactile learner and decides that this stronger sensory modality may need to be employed more effectively in his learning. In discussion with Justin, Chris acknowledges his efforts in learning his weekly spellings but shares her concern that he is not able to commit his learning to long-term memory. They agree to try a different spelling strategy.

Chris teaches Justin to spell 'could'. They begin by writing the word in the air using whole-arm movements in a joined script, saying the letter names. Next Chris encourages Justin to trace the word 'could' first in a tray of sand, and then using a chalk board, always saying the letter names. Finally he writes the word in glitter glue, which he takes home to use again to practise tracing and saying the word. They decide to revise the mantra 'look, cover, write, check' to 'look, say, make, cover, write, check.'

In subsequent sessions, as Justin includes 'would' and 'should' to his spelling list, he makes up a mnemonic, 'o u lucky duck' to add another sensory input to retrieving the 'ould' pattern.

Subsequent analysis of Justin's classwork showed that he was applying his spelling knowledge in his writing and that his standardised spelling score was increasing by approximately 1.5 months spelling age for each month he was on the individualised programme.

In this case study the TA has drawn on her knowledge of learning styles and multi-sensory teaching and observation of Justin's learning style to establish an individual spelling strategy for Justin. This learning strategy includes the utilisation of additional sensory input channels – oral kinaesthetic and tactile kinaesthetic – to enable Justin to more effectively access, store and retrieve new spellings.

Brooks and Weeks (1999) recommended establishing an individual's preferred learning methods to complement the use of multi-sensory teaching materials.

Successful multi-sensory teaching aims to activate two or more pathways simultaneously. This enables the pupil's strongest input channel to take the lead in their learning experience and develops their weaker pathways to learning through their repeated use. This gives pupils greater flexibility in their learning.

Multi-sensory approach to teaching the reading and spelling of irregular words (based on the Fernald Technique and Simultaneous Oral Spelling)

The following method is an example of a multi-sensory approach to teaching pupils how to learn to read and spell a word:

The word should be written large enough to finger-trace.

- The teacher reads the word.
- The teacher traces the letters with the index finger of their dominant hand.
- The teachers says the name of each letter as it is traced.
- The teacher repeats the word.
- The pupil repeats the procedure with the teacher
- The pupil follows the procedure alone.

When the pupil feels confident, the printed word is removed and the pupil writes the word following the same procedure.

The incorporation of articulating letter names and writing the word in a joined script adds two additional sensory inputs to the traditional method of learning spellings through 'look, cover, write and check'.

The Alphabet Arc

abcdefghijklmnopqrstuvwxyz

This is simply the letters of the alphabet arranged in order in a rainbow shape. Each letter can be located easily and the pupil can work in the space under the arc. It appeals particularly to the visual and kinaesthetic learner.

'Alphabet battle' is a way in which two or more pupils can lay out the arc. If two pupils are playing, ensure that one has the 'A' and the other the 'Z'. The pupil who has the 'M' starts the game by placing it in the centre of the arc. The pupils then take it in turns to place letters in sequence either side of the 'M'. The first pupil to place all his letters correctly wins. It is a useful activity that encourages pupils to repeat the alphabet sequence starting at different points. It is important to encourage pupils to articulate the letter names as they place the letters to ensure this is a truly multi-sensory experience.

There are a number of activities which use the alphabet arc to help pupils learn the sequence of the alphabet, identify letters and sounds, segment and blend sounds to make words and generate rhyming analogies, e.g. 'you have made like now make bike'.

A huge variety of tactile letters are available commercially or you can make your own. Learning to lay out the alphabet and using this as the base for teaching letter–sound correspondence is an effective way of employing all the modalities – visual, auditory, tactile kinaesthetic and oral kinaesthetic.

Developing metacognition

'Teach don't tell'. This means teaching your pupils to remember how they remember. It is this metacognitive skill that needs reinforcing. Nisbet and Shucksmith (1986) suggest that successful learners have three traits:

1. they will be acutely aware of their learning style
2. they will be aware of the requirements of each learning situation
3. they will have developed a range of strategies that they can then apply according to their own style.

Good multi-sensory teaching therefore does not focus exclusively on matching teaching style to a pupil's preferred learning style but aims to teach pupils to identify the memory 'hook' that is going to help them access, store and retrieve the information.

As a professional TA you have an important role in ensuring that you teach and prompt pupils to use strategies that enable them to retrieve information when they need it.

PRACTICAL TASK

Identify a pupil who is having a problem remembering a piece of information; for example, their birthday, home address, sequences such as days of the week, a high-frequency word, number bonds, a times table.

Observe them in lessons and talk with them to gain insights into their stronger and weaker learning modalities.

Use your understanding of multi-sensory teaching and knowledge of their learning style, to teach your pupil how to store and retrieve their new knowledge.

Monitor their success in recalling this knowledge or skill daily if possible. Either write a tick if they recall promptly or record a 'P' for practised. Aim to achieve three consecutive ticks in a row but revisit infrequently thereafter. If they are learning a sequence, develop their ability to manipulate the information, for example by asking them to tell you three days before Tuesday. When assessing their recall, ask the pupil either how they remembered.

Summary

While there is little research evidence to support matching teaching to individual pupils' learning styles, multi-sensory teaching can improve their ability to learn and more importantly, engage them more fully in a process of learning *how* to learn:

There is, however, evidence of some consensus as to the value of giving learners the awareness, respectful attention and language to recognise their own best strategies...
(Mortimore 2005)

References

Brooks, P. and Weeks, S. (1999) *Individual Styles in Learning to Spell: Improving Spelling in Children with Literacy Difficulties and all Children in Mainstream Schools*. Nottingham: DfEE Publications.

Burnett, G. (2002) *Learning to Learn*. Carmarthen: Crown House.

Department for Education and Skills (2003) *Excellence and Enjoyment*. London: DfES.

Department for Education and Skills (2004a) *Learning and Teaching for Children with Special Educational Needs in the Primary Years*. London: DfES.

Department for Education and Skills (2004b) *Removing Barriers to Achievement. The Government's Strategy for SEN*. London: DfES.

Gardner, H. (1983) *Multiple Intelligences: The Theory in Practice*. Oxford: Basic Books.

Hughes, M. (2002) *Tweak to Transform. Improving Teaching: A Practical Handbook for School Leaders*. Stafford: Network Educational Press.

Hughes, M. and Vass, A. (2003) *Strategies for Closing the Learning Gap*. Stafford: Network Educational Press.

Lloyd, S. and Wernham, S. (1997) *Using Jolly Phonics – A Guide for Teaching Reading and Writing*. Chigwell: Jolly Learning.

Mortimore, T. (2003) *Dyslexia and Learning Style: A Practitioner's Handbook*. London: Whurr.

Mortimore, T. (2005) Dyslexia and learning style – a note of caution, *British Journal of Special Education*, 32 (3), 145–148.

Muijs, D. (2001) *Effective Teaching. Evidence and Practice*. London: Paul Chapman.

Nisbet, J. and Shucksmith, J. (1986) *Learning Strategies*. London: Routledge and Kegan Paul.

Passy, J. (1993) *Cued Articulation*. Northumberland: Stass Publications.

Shaw, S. and Hawes, T. (1998) *Effective Teaching and Learning in the Primary Classroom*. Leicester: The Services Ltd.

Stahl, S.A. (1999) Different strokes for different folks? A critique of learning styles, *American Educator*, 23 (3), 27–31.

Wood, D. (1988) *How Children Think and Learn*. Oxford: Blackwell.

Zephaniah, B. (2000) *Dyslexia Contact*. London: BDA.

7. Assessment

Introduction

In order to judge the attainment and progress of pupils with SEN, all staff need to work together in the process of observing pupils, recording their attainment/ progress, reporting their achievements to others and monitoring progress over time. Every adult in the classroom is in a position to contribute to this process and provide a useful perspective on pupils' learning and achievements.

In this chapter we will examine some basic principles of assessment and offer practical advice on the assessment cycle. Particular consideration will be given to the use of the P scales, which highlight the progress and attainment of pupils working below age-related expectations. While it is the teacher's responsibility to organise and manage the process of assessment, you have an important role to play in gathering and sharing information. A variety of assessment methods are available and these might range from standardised tests to video depicting attainment in a particular area of the curriculum. Other opportunities may arise through recording progress made towards IEPs, school-based checklists or commercially published materials that focus upon specific areas of development or subject. We must also consider the involvement of pupils themselves in terms of target-setting, self and peer evaluation and celebrating their own achievements. Chapter 9 provides more information on pupil involvement.

HLTA STANDARDS

3.1.2   Working within a framework set by the teacher, they plan their role in lessons including how they will provide feedback to pupils and colleagues on pupils' learning and behaviour.

3.2.1   They are able to support teachers in evaluating pupils' progress through a range of assessment activities.

3.2.2   They monitor pupils' responses to learning tasks and modify their approach accordingly.

3.2.3a They monitor pupils' participation and progress, providing feedback to the teacher.

3.2.3b They monitor pupils' participation and progress, giving constructive support to pupils as they learn.

3.2.4   They contribute to maintaining and analysing records of pupils' progress.

Types of assessment

The two main types of assessment are known as formative assessment (assessment *for* learning) and summative assessment (assessment *of* learning).

Assessment for learning

This is formative in nature and takes place all the time in classrooms and is about using the information gained to improve learning.

Formative assessments may include establishing a pupil's baseline in attainments to gain an understanding of their existing levels of achievement or recording their responses to particular teaching methods, approaches or use of particular resources. This could be recorded in the form of notes on lesson plans which identify how the pupils progressed in the lesson, highlight pupils who had misconceptions or who need more help in understanding concepts or identifying those pupils who may require more challenging tasks.

Other approaches may include:

- targeting specific pupils for observation and recording their progress in lessons or subjects over time
- assessing individual pupils' response to particular programmes or approaches
- assessing pupils' personal interests and key motivators
- assessing against curriculum or individual targets over time in particular areas such as mathematics, reading, writing or gross motor development
- assessing therapeutic needs such as speech and language
- assessing progress towards IEP targets which outline priorities for learning
- pupil self-evaluation, which provides opportunities for pupils to evaluate their achievements against the learning objectives of a particular lesson or series of lessons

- assessing behaviour-related targets
- recording achievement through the use of pupil progress files, including academic, personal, physical or social activities undertaken within the school.

The ways of recording progress and attainment could comprise samples of work, photographs, videotapes, written or taped statements from peers/staff/parents, art/design work or behaviour records. These assessment opportunities may be as a result of a planned activity or at times unexpected. Therefore, assessment for learning should become an integral part of the teaching and learning process and involve a range of adults within the classroom.

> *Assessment for learning is the process of seeking and interpreting evidence for use by learners and their teachers to decide where the learners are in their learning, where they need to go and how best to get there.* (Assessment Reform Group and QCA 2002)

Assessment of learning

This type of assessment is summative in nature and may take place at certain times during the academic year. It represents a snapshot which demonstrates what a pupil can do at that particular moment in time.

These assessments may include:

- National statutory tests taken at the end of a key stage, or voluntary national tests taken at the ends of Years 3, 4, and 5.
- P-scale performance descriptions which are related to all pupils aged between 5 and 16 who have learning difficulties. This includes pupils who are unlikely to achieve above Level 2 at Key Stage 4 and pupils who may be working at age-related expectations in some subjects but are well below this in others.
- Baseline tests which are undertaken on pupil entry to school.
- The Foundation Stage Profile, which is based upon practitioners' ongoing observations and assessments in all six areas of learning.
- Commercially produced tests which are purchased by schools, for example Salford reading or Vernon spelling tests.
- School- or class-based tests written by practitioners and used to establish general attainment or to make interim judgements about progress.

Short-term planning and assessment

Assessment is likely to be effective if the learning outcomes or intentions are clear and this will involve differentiation for individuals or groups of pupils. Pupils with SEN may be working at very different levels and have individual support needs that have to be considered. In this respect it is helpful to consider the three principles for inclusion within the *National Curriculum Handbook 2000* which relate to assessment.

Setting suitable learning challenges

- to take account of any gaps in pupils' learning resulting from missed or interrupted schooling
- for pupils whose attainments fall significantly below the expected levels at a particular key stage.

Responding to pupils' diverse learning needs

Teachers should use appropriate assessment approaches that:

- take account of different learning styles
- provide clear and unambiguous feedback to pupils to aid their learning.

Overcoming potential barriers to learning and assessment for individuals and groups of pupils

The *National Curriculum Handbook* states that 'Curriculum planning and assessment for pupils with SEN must take account of the type and extent of the difficulty experienced by the pupil.' Therefore, the short-term plan should be a working document that all staff working within the classroom has access to. It should outline the activities to be undertaken, organisation of those activities, a breakdown of the learning intentions including differentiation, the role of the additional adults within the activity and the expected outcomes for individuals or groups of pupils. They might also include curricular targets which relate to specific elements of a subject. These targets maybe related to the National Literacy Strategy or National Numeracy Strategy target statements or elements identified by the teacher. In the Foundation stage, targets are more likely to be informed by a shared understanding of what a pupil can do.

In the busy classroom TAs sometimes find themselves working independently with particular groups or individuals with little time to share information about progress or achievements. It is essential that opportunities are provided for TAs to listen, observe and engage with pupils in order to check their understanding. It is important to provide verbal and written feedback to the teacher on how far pupils were successful in meeting the learning intentions of the lesson and about any difficulties experienced, including suggestions for future teaching; in some cases this may mean opportunities to revisit a learning objective but with activities and materials presented in different ways.

Recording

Records need to be written in a language that is clear and unambiguous and should:

- be focused and informative rather than descriptive
- provide information about why pupils might be experiencing difficulties
- focus on pupils' strengths as well as weaknesses.

Recognising progress and achievement

All pupils, including those with SEN, demonstrate progress in terms of increased knowledge, skills and understanding. Sometimes this may be lateral progress rather than hierarchical, with very small steps in learning, for example, pupils may:

- Develop a range of responses to social interactions from defensiveness through resistance (for some pupils, a positive response) to tolerance; and from passive co-operation towards active participation with individuals, in groups and in wider social circumstances.
- Develop a range of responses to actions, events or experiences even if there is no clear progress in acquiring knowledge and skills.
- Demonstrate the same achievement on more than one occasion and under changing circumstances.
- Demonstrate an increase in knowledge and understanding about a subject.
- Demonstrate an ability to maintain, refine, generalise or combine skills over time and in a range of circumstances, situations and settings.
- Move from a dependence on secure and predictable routines towards a greater degree of autonomy shown by risk-taking and increased confidence.
- Demonstrate a reduced need for support, for example, from another person, from technology, from individualised equipment, in carrying out particular tasks.
- Develop a wider regular use of learning positions and learning environments, reducing the need to present activities in consistent and personalised ways.
- Show a reduction in the frequency or severity of behaviour that inhibits learning through more appropriate behaviour.
- Demonstrate an increased ability to cope, for example, with frustration and failure, with new or challenging learning opportunities or situations.
- Decide not to participate or to respond.

Staff need to recognise that, because of their learning difficulties, some pupils may reach a plateau in their achievements, or regress. This is usually temporary, but sometimes can be lengthy or permanent. In such cases, pupils' recorded attainments, or achievements previously predicted by staff, may decline. A slowing of the rate of regression, shown by skills or capabilities being maintained or reactivated, is then a form of progress.

Recognising attainment for pupils with learning difficulties

Planning, Teaching and Assessing the Curriculum for Pupils with Learning Difficulties: Recognising Attainment (QCA 2001) provides a useful framework to help teachers recognise attainment below the level of the National Curriculum. It describes possible changes in individual pupils' responses and behaviour as their early perceptions of experiences and their increasing involvement in the learning process develop into areas of knowledge, skills and understanding. The development of internal learning processes, for example, thinking skills, is shown by degrees of attention, discrimination and participation in experiences and activities.

A framework for recognising attainment
Encounter Pupils are present during an experience or activity without any obvious learning outcome, although for some pupils, for example, those who withhold their attention or their presence from many situations, their willingness to tolerate a shared activity may, in itself, be significant.
Awareness Pupils appear to show awareness that something has happened and notice, fleetingly focus on or attend to an object, event or person, for example, by briefly interrupting a pattern of self-absorbed movement or vocalisation.
Attention and response Pupils attend and begin to respond, often not consistently, to what is happening, for example, by showing signs of surprise, enjoyment, frustration or dissatisfaction, demonstrating the beginning of an ability to distinguish between different people, objects, events and places.
Engagement Pupils show more consistent attention to, and can tell the difference between, specific events in their surroundings, for example, by focused looking or listening; turning to locate objects, events or people; following moving objects and events through movements of their eyes, head or other body parts.
Participation Pupils engage in sharing, taking turns and the anticipation of familiar sequences of events, for example, by smiling, vocalising or showing other signs of excitement, although these responses may be supported by staff or other pupils.
Involvement Pupils actively strive to reach out, join in or comment in some way on the activity itself or on the actions or responses of the other pupils, for example, by making exploratory hand and arm movements, seeking eye contact with staff or other pupils, or by speaking, signing or gesturing.
Gaining skills and understanding Pupils gain, strengthen or make general use of their skills, knowledge, concepts or understanding that relate to their experience of the curriculum, for example, they can recognise the features of an object and understand its relevance, significance and use.

(QCA 2001)

Using the P scales to recognise attainment and progress

The P scales provide an assessment criteria for progress below Level 1 of the National Curriculum programmes of study and were initially developed to support the target-setting process. The P scales have filled a gap in recognising the attainment of pupils working below Level 1 of the National Curriculum levels of attainment and replace the use of 'W', which indicated that pupils were working towards National Curriculum Level 1. They are designed for pupils aged 5–16 and represent summative assessments that can be used at the end of each year or end of key stage. They are commonly used within the special school context but should be used in a more inclusive way to support pupils across all schools.

The P scales were not written for pupils in the Foundation stage and in this respect the Foundation Stage Profile is statutory and must be completed for all pupils in the early years. The DfES notes that if pupils aged 3–5 years have obvious learning difficulties and are likely to receive a statement of SEN, then there may be a purpose in using P scales P1–P3 for some early assessments.

The P scales are informed by teacher assessment and should be a 'best fit' judgement that can track linear progress over a period of time towards Level 1 of the National Curriculum. There are a number of commercial packages that support the P scale process, such as PACE by EQUALS, Pivats or B Squared. As a professional TA you may find yourself (in collaboration with a teacher) using the P scales to assess pupils working outside the National Curriculum.

P scale descriptions are available in the following core subjects and strands:

English	Speaking	Listening	Reading	Writing
Mathematics	Shape, space and measure	Number	Using and applying mathematics	
Science				
ICT				

P scales are also available within the Qualifications and Curriculum Authority (QCA) for each National Curriculum subject plus PSHE, citizenship and RE.

Do remember the following about the structure and organisation of the P scales:

- P1–P3 are common across all subjects, although some subject-focused examples are included to illustrate some of the ways in which staff might identify attainment in different subject contexts.
- P4–P8 are written to include the emergence of skills, knowledge and understanding in specific subjects and the descriptions provide examples of these.

Involving pupils in assessment

Involving pupils in developing the skills of self-assessment is important if they are to understand their own learning. This may well start with the sharing of the learning intentions, objectives and success criteria.

In this process it is helpful to think about the language used:

'We are learning to...' when referring to learning objectives.

'Remember to...' when referring to success criteria.

Another way might be saying to the pupils 'The thing I am looking for is...' or 'the reasons you are doing this is to find more about...' (DfES 2004)

Additional strategies for sharing the learning intentions might include writing the learning intentions on the whiteboard using different colours to highlight particular words, reminding pupils throughout the lesson and checking that they know what the learning intentions are through the use of pictorial or symbolic visual cues.

Involving pupils by providing effective feedback

Pupils need to be encouraged to speak freely about their learning and ways to demonstrate their understanding. Approaches to consider may include:

- oral feedback focused on the learning intentions and outcomes
- using pupils' contributions within the whole class or group
- written feedback which includes brief useful comments linked to the success criteria, focusing on elements of success, with one or two suggestions for improvement.

It is important that we teach pupils to reflect on their learning and develop the skills to communicate their thoughts about their work and progress to us. Research has shown that developing these skills can improve attainment and achievement and have a positive effect on self-esteem. This can be undertaken verbally by asking and developing effective questioning. A good set of questions could include the following:

- What did you find easy?
- What did you find difficult/where did you get stuck? What helped you to get out of the difficulty? (Was it something a friend said or did, something the teacher did, something to do with equipment, something you did yourself?)
- What do you need more help with?
- What are you most pleased with?
- Have you learnt anything new?
- How would you change this activity for another group/class?
- Do you have any questions?

(Clarke 2003)

This type of approach to questioning will require modelling by the teacher or yourself to provide examples of the different responses that pupils might give, if pupils are to acquire these skills and develop the confidence to explore these ways of thinking about their work.

Marking of work can also provide effective feedback providing it is linked to the learning objectives and success criteria. It also needs to demonstrate areas in which the pupil has succeeded and where improvement could be made, including strategies for improvement where relevant. When working with pupils with SEN, consideration needs to be given to the use of meaningful language when providing oral feedback, visual prompts such as symbols, pictures to enhance written feedback and ensuring that time is taken to provide the right amount of feedback. Other pupils may require alternatives such as pictorial/symbolic mind maps, tape recording, video recording, displays, oral presentations or the use of ICT.

Other assessment opportunities could include providing opportunities for peer and self-assessment in which pupils are encouraged to reflect upon their own work or that of others.

Monitoring

Monitoring is used at whole-school level to ensure consistency and continuity in assessment and pupil progress. In your role as a TA you are likely to use the IEP as a tool for monitoring individual pupil progress. It is important to gather the views of the pupil, parents and other relevant professionals.

If monitoring is to be effective, the information gathered needs to be used to inform new targets and where progress has not been made, further analysis and the implementation of alternative programmes and strategies may be needed.

Target-setting

Individual targets need to outline the next most achievable stage in particular areas of learning and these need to be explored and agreed with the pupil. They need to include priorities in learning and targets that the pupil is close to achieving. Individual targets need to be:

- easily recognised by the pupil and visible
- understood by all additional adults working in the classroom
- threaded through a range of learning activities
- subject to regular feedback
- shared with parents/carers in order to promote interest at home
- be achievable; and if no progress is evident then think about the appropriateness of the target and if it needs to be modified.

If targets are well written and appropriate, pupils will be motivated to work towards their targets and to develop confidence in being able to identify and say what their future targets should be.

Summary

The real value of assessment lies in identifying where pupils are in their learning in order to inform appropriate learning targets, strategies and programmes. The professional TA often works more closely and frequently with a pupil and is therefore able to contribute information not only about assessment and task outcomes but also observations about the pupil's interests, motivation, persistence and responsiveness to support.

References

Assessment Reform Group (1998) *Testing, Motivation and Learning*. Cambridge: University of Cambridge School of Education.

Assessment Reform Group (1999) *Assessment for Learning: Beyond the Black Box*. Cambridge: University of Cambridge School of Education.

Assessment Reform Group (2002) *Assessment for Learning: 10 Principles*. Cambridge: University of Cambridge School of Education.

Black, P. and Wiliam, D. (1998) *Inside the Black Box: Raising Standards through Classroom Assessment*. London: King's College London School of Education.

Black, P., Harrison, C., Lee, C., Marshall, B. and Wiliam, D. (2002) *Working Inside the Black Box: Assessment for Learning in the Classroom*. London: King's College London School of Education.

Clarke, S. (1998a) *Targeting Assessment in the Primary Classroom: Strategies for Planning, Assessment, Pupil Feedback, and Target Setting*. London: Hodder & Stoughton.

Clarke, S. (1998b) *Unlocking Formative Assessment: Practical Strategies for Enhancing Pupils' Learning in the Primary Classroom*. London: Hodder & Stoughton.

Clarke, S. (2003) *Enriching Feedback in the Primary Classroom*. London: Hodder & Stoughton

Department for Education and Skills (2004) *Primary National Strategy. Excellence and Enjoyment. Learning and Teaching in the Primary Years: Assessment for learning*. London: DfES.

Gross, J. (2003) *Special Educational Needs and School Improvement: Practical Strategies for Raising Standards*. London: David Fulton.

Qualifications and Curriculum Authority (2001) *Planning, Teaching and Assessing the Curriculum for Pupils with Learning Difficulties*. London: QCA.

Acknowledgements

The East Midlands SEN Partnership – Supporting the use of the P Scales in the East Midlands Region (Fergusson, A., Green, J. and Leeson, S.) EMSEN/University of Northampton.

Fairfield Special School, Northampton

Elizabeth Lewin, Adviser for Curriculum Assessment Key Stage 1 – NIAS

8. Working in partnership

Introduction

The education of pupils with SEN usually involves working in partnership with parents/carers and a range of professionals and external agencies. They all play a vital role in the provision of information about the pupil and providing teaching strategies or interventions to assist learning. As a TA you will find yourself having frequent contact with parents/carers and implementing specific teaching approaches or programmes under the direction of a range of professionals. The value of these partnerships is important and in this chapter we will examine some useful strategies and approaches to aid effective communication, information sharing and working relationships with other professionals.

A workable definition of partnership is provided by Gascoigne (1995):

- each partner recognises the different skills, experiences and knowledge of each of the other partners
- each partner values the skills, experiences and knowledge of each of the other partners
- all partners recognise the need for the input of each of the partners
- each partner feels valued.

HLTA STANDARDS

1.4   They work collaboratively with colleagues, and carry out their roles effectively knowing when to seek help and advice.

1.5   They are able to liaise sensitively and effectively with parents and carers, recognising their role in pupils' learning.

2.1   They have sufficient understanding of their specialist area to support pupils' learning, and are able to acquire further knowledge to contribute effectively and with confidence to the classes in which they are involved.

2.8   They know the legal definition of Special Education Needs (SEN), and are familiar with the guidance about meeting SEN given in the SEN Code of Practice.

3.2.1   They are able to support teachers in evaluating pupils' progress through a range of assessment activities.

3.2.2   They monitor pupils' responses to learning tasks and modify their approach accordingly.

3.2.4   They contribute to maintaining and analysing records of pupils' progress.

3.3.5 They advance pupil's learning in a range of classroom settings, including working with individual pupils, small groups and whole classes.

3.3.6 They are able, where relevant, to guide the work of other adults supporting teaching and learning in the classroom.

CHAPTER OBJECTIVES

By the end of this chapter you should:

- have considered some of the issues for working in partnership as identified in the SEN Code of Practice

- be aware of the difficulties faced by many parents/carers of children with SEN

- have an understanding of support services that are available to help parents and carers

- be aware of the role of the SENCo and how TAs can support their work

- have considered the role of other professionals in meeting the learning needs of pupils with SEN.

Partnership with parents/carers

The development of partnerships with parents/carers has increased throughout the last 20 years as they have been perceived as consumers who have entitlement to choice and participation in the education of their children. Since the 1990s schools have been required to inform parents about their developments, policies and practices. In 2001 the revised SEN Code of Practice devoted a chapter to 'Working in partnership with parents'.

Partnership with parents plays a key role in promoting a culture of co-operation between parents, schools, LEAs and others. This is important in enabling children and young people with SEN to achieve their potential.

(DfES 2001)

This statement recognises the key role of parents/carers in the education of their child. It recognises that they hold key information and have a variety of unique skills, knowledge and understanding of their child that can contribute to a shared view of a child's needs. The Code of Practice states that parents/carers should be supported and empowered to:

- recognise and fulfil their responsibilities as parents and play an active and valued role in their children's education
- have knowledge of their entitlement within the SEN framework
- make their views known about how their child is educated

- have access to information, advice and support during assessment and any related decision-making processes about special educational provision.

The SEN Code of Practice also ensured the provision of access by parents/carers to an independent parental supporter for all who want one. Parent partnership services can be found in most local education authorities and are a statutory service that offers information, advice and support for parents/carers of children and young people with SEN. They have a role in making sure that parent's views are heard and understood by all concerned through the provision of impartial advice.

A parental supporter can assist parents and carers by listening to their worries and concerns or helping them to express their views. A parent/carer might ask them to help make phone calls, fill in forms and write letters or reports. They could attend meetings and help to resolve disagreements about SEN matters as well as providing general and ongoing support. A crucial part of their role is supporting parents during statutory assessment which may result in the issuing of a statement of special educational need and in the annual reviews of statements.

Case study

Simran is a Year 2 pupil who has recently joined a new primary school after moving into the area. He has a statement of Special Educational Needs and has moderate learning difficulties and visual impairment, with particular difficulties in literacy and numeracy. His mother often talks to the TA about how his day has been when collecting him from school. On one occasion his mother mentions that she is worried about his coming review meeting. She is unsure of the process, finds such meetings daunting and has difficulty in expressing her views in such a meeting. The TA discusses this with the class teacher and SENCo, who talk with the parent. They provide the parent with information about the local parent partnership service and discuss their role in supporting parents/carers. The mother contacts the service, who arrange for someone to visit the home. They speak with the parents about the annual review process and the parent asks them to attend the meeting and allow some time after the meeting to discuss the outcomes. The review meeting takes place and the parent feels far more knowledgeable about the process, has a clear idea of what she wants to say, feels supported during the meeting and understands the implications of the outcomes and actions following the meeting.

Identification and diagnosis of SEN

This is often an extremely difficult time for parents/carers and as a TA you need to be aware of the emotional impact upon the family and how to offer appropriate support.

What are the issues for parents with children with SEN?

This includes the initial discovery that their child has SEN and the uncertainty of what arrangements will be made to support the child and the family. Multi-agency involvement can sometimes be difficult to accept and parents/carers often talk about being immersed in professional language that everyone is using which they don't understand, or that they have to keep repeating the story about their child's difficulties to so many different people.

The problems of labelling the child as having special educational needs and the implications of the SEN Code of Practice in themselves can be daunting.

In 2003 Mencap produced a report called *No Ordinary Life*, which focused on pupils with severe and profound and multiple learning difficulties. It describes the feelings and experience of many parents/carers. It found that:

- the caring role places an enormous strain upon the family
- the support given to families can be variable and at times very limited
- diagnosis can be an extremely difficult time.

   'You cannot attend to the aches and pains of old age, or allow yourself to think about them.'

   'To be ill is not possible. However you feel, you have to carry on.'

Ways to support partnerships with parents and carers

This section will explore ways in which TAs can support parents/carers and the work of the school. Listen to what parents/carers have to say: it may provide an opportunity to build a cumulative picture of the pupil's abilities and needs. Parents/carers can often provide key information about communication, behaviour, health and their child's routines and habits – this will help you to become consistent in your approach. We need to accept that parents/carers will usually know their child better than anyone. Take their concerns seriously and if appropriate share any concerns with the class teacher or SENCo.

Recognise the emotional impact of having a child with SEN and remember that parents/carers may come from a different perspective. They may find it hard to accept that their child has special needs or feel that they need to fight to get the best provision for their child. Do not label parents/carers as difficult, because they may be confused, angry, hurt or emotionally exhausted.

Remember that part of your role is to develop a positive relationship and to foster links between home and school. At times you may be required to be a 'listening ear' in order to support parents. This can be difficult and at times it may be necessary to avoid getting embroiled in more complex issues. Think about the language we use and that professionals tend to talk in code that parents/carers find difficult to understand. Talk to parents/carers in jargon-free language or help to explain what terms mean if they are unsure.

Parents/carers often feel that they would like to do more for their child at home; if this is the case talk with the class teacher or SENCo. Do bear in mind that many parents/carers are new to this situation and will usually want to support their child as much as possible. In other situations you may feel that parents/carers could do more. Try not to be judgemental as there may be many different reasons why this is difficult. When discussing the child with the parent/carer, use active listening skills and remember to focus on the child's abilities, not just their difficulties.

Find out if the school has a key worker or mentor system which could help the pupil make a stronger emotional attachment to a key member of staff and help parents/carers to share more information and ask for advice. Do think carefully about issues of confidentiality as you are likely to have access to oral and written information from parents/carers, other colleagues and professionals. This information may be helpful in managing the learning of the pupil, but may need to be kept within the classroom team. Remember that parents/carers may not want certain bits of information shared with others. Unprofessional or judgemental comments overheard about a child or parent/carer could damage a trusting relationship and be very difficult to repair. Finally, celebrate the achievements of both the child and the parents/carers.

> *Parents are the children's first and most enduring educators. When parents and practitioners work together in early year's settings, the results have a positive impact on the child's development and learning. Therefore, each setting should seek to develop an effective partnership with parents.*
>
> (QCA 2000)

Working in partnership with the SENCo and teachers

The SEN Code of Practice describes the SENCo as the member of staff of a school or early years setting who has responsibility for co-ordinating SEN provision within that school. The key role of the SENCo is to support the head teacher and governing body, by taking responsibility for the day-to-day operation of provision made by the school for pupils with SEN and providing professional guidance to all staff in the areas of SEN. In many cases the management of TAs to support pupils with SEN has become a key responsibility of the SENCo. You may find that you are in the position of being managed by a SENCo, working for large parts of the day in one class, supporting pupils with SEN across the school or working with an individual pupil for most of the day.

Using TAs effectively is not an easy task for most teachers; if work is unfocused then the benefits of additional adults within the classroom are not maximised. Good classroom management and working arrangements with TAs can make a difference to the quality of support for pupils and enable TAs to work more productively with pupils. As a TA it is important that you feel supported and confident in meeting the needs of the individuals and groups that you work with; if not, it is important to ask for support or training.

Case study

The TA has been asked by the SENCo to implement the Catch Up programme, a structured literacy intervention strategy for pupils aged 6 to 11 years following joint training by Catch Up consultants. The TA assesses the literacy skills and attitude to reading of pupils identified by the SENCo, using the materials in the pupil progress booklet. Together they discuss the outcomes of the assessment and select pupils who will benefit from the scheme. The TA teaches the programme and keeps a record of each session in the pupil progress booklet so that everyone helping the pupil can keep up to date with their progress. The SENCo and TA review the pupils' progress each week.

The above approach echoes the work of Crown (2003b), who notes that teachers and other adults working together in classrooms need training opportunities to develop good teamwork and communication.

Working with teachers

This can be a sensitive area and one that requires professionalism and a relationship built on mutual respect. The role of HLTA has added another dimension to the part played by the TA and you will find yourself more involved in learning and teaching, assessment, monitoring and planning. It would be useful if class teachers were aware of your experience if undertaking the assessment only route or the requirements of the taught route in order to understand the types of experience or training that you have.

Regular opportunities for planning, discussion and feedback need to become a regular feature of the working week and this could involve differentiation in planning, reviewing IEPs, preparing resources, direction of additional adults and monitoring and recording of lesson outcomes and pupil progress. In relation to feedback it is essential to agree when this will occur, what should be recorded and how information should be fed back to the teacher.

Balshaw *et al.* (1999) identified some important principles underpinning successful working relationships, including:

- clearly defined roles and responsibilities
- opportunities to communicate, e.g. joint planning, and regular meetings for discussion and evaluation
- consistency of approach in the management of the learning in terms of expectations, planning and classroom organisation
- opportunities to continue professional development and participate in performance reviews.

If these principles are taken into account then you are more likely to feel valued and supported in your role as a professional TA working effectively with colleagues to manage the learning and teaching of all pupils.

Managing the work of additional adults

As part of the HLTA Standard 3.3.6 you may find that part of your role involves the direction and supervision of additional adults within the classroom. This is an aspect of your role that will need to be managed sensitively but effectively to assist pupils in their learning. Strategies that promote effective partnerships include:

- involving additional adults in planning and ensuring that they have opportunities to look at plans and ask any questions in advance of the lesson
- making sure that they are clear about their role in the lesson and have access to the appropriate resources
- providing regular opportunities to feed back on the pupils' learning
- having time to discuss individual pupils.

PRACTICAL TASK

Complete the following checklist in relation to the school in which you work. Where you cannot fill in the boxes, ask the SENCo or teacher from your school for the information.

Ways to support partnerships with the SENCo and teachers

ASPECTS OF THE TA'S ROLE	EVIDENCE
I am familiar with key school policies and procedures	
I am aware of roles and responsibilities and procedures for communicating with parents, teachers and other professionals. This may include establishing ground rules for the management of behaviour or working as a team.	
I have a clear understanding about communication systems of the class or school and my involvement in team meetings, staff meeting, or meeting with the SENCo/teacher.	
I have a clear understanding of my role and input into annual review or other meetings with parents and other professionals.	
I have spoken with and understand the role of the SENCo.	
I am aware of the IEPs or behaviour support plans for the pupils I work with including my role in supporting their learning.	
I am clear about my role in monitoring and recording pupil progress with the pupil/s I support in terms of their work IEPs or behaviour plans.	

I am aware of the learning support needs of the pupils I work with. I have access to useful information about my pupil/s and understand if they are on School Action, School Action Plus or have statement and understand what this means.	
My professional development needs are known and I have opportunities to attend in-service training opportunities.	
I am involved in performance management systems within my school.	
The SENCo and teacher are aware of my skills and experience.	
I am sure about my role in supporting learning and the development of independence, self help and study skills for the pupil/s I work with.	

Working in partnership with other professionals

The SEN Code of Practice states that all services for pupils with SEN should focus on identifying and addressing the needs of pupils and enabling them to improve their situation through:

- early identification
- continual engagement with the pupil and carers/parents
- focused intervention
- dissemination of effective approaches and techniques.

As a TA working with pupils who have SEN you are bound to come across a range of other professionals. The principles we have described above for working with teachers, parents and the SENCo apply equally to working with other colleagues. Other professionals, such as speech therapists, psychologists or support teachers, have specific responsibilities with which you need to become familiar. When asked to work alongside these colleagues you should continue to take advice from teachers and ensure that you note any actions which may be required for specific pupils.

Summary

You are likely to find yourself working closely with parents and other professionals who may simply find you either easier to talk to or more accessible because you are working with the pupil on a daily basis. It is important to be able to listen, take advice and communicate and share information sensitively with all relevant parties, maintaining confidentiality.

References

Balshaw, M., Farrell, P. and Polat, F. (1999) *The Management, Role and Training of Learning Support Assistants*. Nottingham: DfES.

Cheminais, R. (2001) *Developing Inclusive School Practice – A Practical Guide*. London: David Fulton.

Crowne, E. (2003a) *Developing Inclusive School Practice – The SENCo's Role in Managing Change*. London: David Fulton.

Crowne, E. (2003b) *The SENCo Handbook – Working Within a Whole School Approach*. London: David Fulton.

Department for Education and Skills (2001) *Special Educational Needs – Code of Practice*. London: DfES.

Department for Education and Skills (2002) *Together from the Start – Practical Guidance for Professionals Working with Disabled Children (Birth to 2) and Their Families*. London: DfES.

Department for Education and Skills (2003a) *Excellence and Enjoyment*. London: DfES.

Department for Education and Skills (2003b) *Materials for Schools – Involving Parents, Raising Achievement*. London: DfES.

Department for Education and Skills (2004) *Removing Barriers to Achievement – The Government's Strategy for SEN*. London: DfES.

Fox, G. (2003) *A Handbook for Learning Support Assistants*. London: David Fulton.

Gascoigne, E. (1995) *Working with Parents as Partners in SEN*. London: David Fulton.

George, J. and Hunt, M. (2003) *Appointing and Managing Learning Support Assistants*. London: David Fulton.

Halliwell, M. (2003) *Supporting Children with Special Educational Needs – A Guide for Assistants in Schools and Pre-Schools*. London: David Fulton.

Mencap (2003) *No Ordinary Life*. London: Mencap.

Ramjhun, A. (2002) *Implementing the Code of Practice for Children with Special Educational Needs*. London: David Fulton.

9. Pupil involvement

Introduction

Bennathan (1996) notes the advantages that can be gained from high levels of pupil involvement in all aspects of learning. These include increased pupil autonomy and moving towards independence. In the case of pupils with SEN, there are different views on the extent to which pupils are capable of contributing to their own learning or involvement in decision-making. These views are usually based upon what constitutes capability, appropriate age, maturity and levels of understanding.

In this chapter we will investigate ways in which TAs can work with teachers to involve pupils in their learning, including those with SEN. It is important not to assume that because a pupil has SEN they cannot or should not be involved in aspects of their own learning.

The Convention on the Rights of the Child (Article 12) states that:

> parties shall assure to the child who is capable of forming his or her own views the right to express those views freely in all matters affecting the child, the views of the child being given due weight in accordance with the age and maturity of the child.   (United Nations 1989)

All pupils need to develop effective learning strategies in order to analyse and interpret information and use these skills to problem-solve and make decisions. Pupils with learning difficulties are likely to face a greater challenge in gaining these skills and understanding. They may face additional obstacles in the form of low expectations or tokenism on the part of some staff, difficulties in communication, being open to suggestibility or dependency.

The Special Educational Needs Code of Practice (2001) notes that:

> there is a fine balance between giving the child a voice and encouraging them to make informed decisions, and overburdening them with decision-making procedures where they have insufficient experience and knowledge to make appropriate judgements.

The above statement is important because it reminds us of the difficulties faced by some pupils and the notion that some of the skills and understanding required to make informed choice and decisions may need to be discreetly taught rather than acquired naturally. It also establishes the importance of having high expectations and attitudes towards involving pupils with special educational needs in their learning.

The Code also recognises the rights of pupils to be involved in the decision-making process in schools and provides them with opportunities to express their views and aspirations. It contains a separate chapter on pupil involvement which states that pupils:

should, where possible, participate in all decision making processes that occur in education including the setting of learning targets and contributing to IEPs, discussions about choice of schools, contributing to the assessment of their needs and to the annual review and transition process. They should feel confident that they will be listened to and that their views are valued.

HLTA STANDARDS

1.1   They have high expectations of all pupils; respect their social, cultural, linguistic, religious, and ethnic backgrounds; and are committed to raising their educational achievement.

1.2   They build and maintain successful relationships with pupils, treat them consistently, with respect and consideration for their development as learners.

2.8   They know the legal definition of Special Education Needs (SEN), and are familiar with the guidance about meeting SEN given in the SEN Code of Practice.

3.1.2   Working within a framework set by the teacher, they plan their role in lessons, including how they will provide feedback to pupils and colleagues on pupils' learning and behaviour.

3.2.3   They monitor pupils' participation and progress, providing feedback to teachers, and giving constructive support to pupils as they learn.

3.3.2   They communicate effectively and sensitively with pupils to support their learning.

CHAPTER OBJECTIVES

By the end of this chapter you should:

● be aware of what we mean by pupil involvement

● understand why we should involve pupils

● understand how we can involve pupils and useful strategies to promote this

● consider how pupils can learn to be involved.

What do we mean by pupil involvement?

Pupils with SEN may be involved at different levels and in different ways. It may take the form of involvement in setting targets and learning objectives within IEPs, including monitoring, recording and evaluation. It should also include involvement within the statutory assessment process, attendance and contribution to the annual review process or the transition process when moving schools or leaving school at an appropriate level for the pupil. Curriculum involvement could include pupils being taught thinking and organisational skills or developing the key skills of communication.

Planning, Teaching and Assessing the Curriculum for Pupils with Learning Difficulties (QCA 2001) provides guidance on supporting and developing the curriculum for pupils with SEN and focuses on the development of key skills, thinking skills and additional skills which may form further priority areas of learning. Other features may include becoming involved in assessing, recording and monitoring of their own learning, for example, as part of setting and reviewing subject targets. Finally, pupils could participate in the wider life of the school such as a school council or through contributing to aspects of the school improvement plan.

Case study

Joseph is a Year 1 pupil who has cerebral palsy. He vocalises in response to adults but his sounds are not yet recognisable as words. In consultation with his parents and the speech and language therapist, he has been provided with a speech-input tool which helps him communicate his needs and ideas, organise them, and make choices. A boy's voice of the same age is used to record the words and phrases that Joseph needs. He chooses them by pressing the right pad in response to requests and comments. The speech and language therapist supports staff and parents in helping Joseph to use the device and select the most appropriate words and phrases.

(From QCA 2001)

Why is pupil participation important?

Recent literature has indicated that pupil participation is important because it is successful in promoting independence and organisational/study skills; develops pupil self-esteem and confidence; and assists pupils to develop assertiveness skills. Teachers' and TAs' relationships with pupils are improved, which can lead to improved patterns of behaviour and greater motivation in learning and expressing their opinions. In relation to learning, pupils are more committed to achievements, have high expectations enabling pupils to be seen as part of the learning community. Munby (1995), who reviewed pupil participation in the assessment process, states:

> *we need to involve students in the assessment process not only because it is more likely to motivate them as learners, not only because students should be entitled to such an involvement, but also because, when done well, it can save the teacher time and make the process more manageable. Moreover, involving students in their own assessment is more likely to lead to accurate judgements about their attainments.*

Participation in the target-setting process and IEPs

Pupils need to understand about the process of IEPs and target-setting. We should not take it for granted that they understand why they have IEPs or the significance of their objectives or targets. TAs are in an ideal position to help them, as they have usually developed a close and positive relationship with the pupil. IEPs and targets need to be discussed with pupils and they should be encouraged to discuss their strengths and weaknesses. They may need to understand the difference between long- and short-term targets and understand their role in recording, monitoring and evaluating their targets. We should certainly provide opportunities for pupils to suggest their own targets and this could include the use of visual cues such pictures, photographs or symbols to illustrate targets. Pupils may need to discuss strategies to help them achieve their targets and recognise any particular difficulties and how they can overcome any barriers to learning, including the support they will need to do this. Ownership of IEPs and targets is essential if pupils are to feel involved, recognise their achievements and reach their targets. They need to have a copy of their IEP presented in ways that they can understand and contribute towards.

We need to be aware that the language used by staff in the IEP target-setting sessions may be both an encouraging and inhibiting factor in enabling pupils to play a full role. Finally, we need to remember that in order for pupils to gain confidence in setting targets we need to find ways to teach them to develop these skills and provide support, including the most appropriate person to work with the pupil.

PRACTICAL TASK

In order to complete this task you will need to negotiate some time with your teacher to look at and discuss the IEP of pupils with whom you are familiar. Review the targets within the IEP with the teacher and include the following in your discussions about the targets within the IEP.

- Are pupils involved in IEP review meetings?
- How is the IEP/target-setting process shared with the pupil?
- In what ways is the pupil involved in developing the IEP targets?
- What part does the pupil have in examining their strengths and areas for development including ways to overcome barriers to learning?
- In what ways are the IEP targets communicated to the pupil so that they are able to understand them?
- Does the pupil have a copy of their IEP targets?
- How is the pupil involved in recording, monitoring and evaluating their IEP targets?

Together think about the following: are there any ways that the IEP target-setting process could be further developed to aid pupil involvement or access?

Pupil involvement in the formal review process

The SEN Code of Practice notes that the annual review process provides an opportunity for pupils with SEN to express their views and take part in decisions about their education. Where pupils are present at annual review or other meetings, they need to understand what the meeting will be about, who will be present, and what kinds of things will be discussed and their part within the meeting.

Prior to the meeting

Following discussion with the pupil we need to decide upon their attendance. It is important to take into account the feelings of the pupil and be sensitive to the content of the discussion in order to make it a positive experience for the pupil. This may mean that the pupil attends for some of the meeting – usually the beginning, leaving some time for professionals to have additional discussion time if required. We also need to think about who will support the pupil with their contributions. This might be a parent, friend, advocate or TA who has a special relationship with the pupil. If this is the case then you will need to prepare carefully for the meeting with the pupil in order to decide the best ways to do this.

During the meeting

As a TA attending the meeting you will need to make sure that the pupil understands what is being said by others and at times you may find that you need to interpret information for the pupil. They need to be provided with time to think and respond and this might involve giving the pupil opportunities to ask further questions. Wherever possible we need to avoid jargon, negative questions, double-barrelled questions, over-intrusive style of questioning and complex language. Strategies such as role play and rehearsal might help to provide the pupil with the skills and confidence to contribute successfully.

After the meeting

This is an important part of the process and should not be discounted. It provides ways of ensuring the pupil's understanding and checking for mixed or confused messages. As a TA you may find yourself providing feedback to the pupil about the meeting and making sure that they understand the key issues and the implications of any decisions.

Pupils who do not attend the meeting

We also need to consider how we work with those pupils who do not wish to or who are unable to attend the meetings. The strategies we could employ might involve:

- providing information through visual methods, for example video, photographs, symbols or samples of work

- asking an advocate or friend to report discussions and key messages with the pupil on their behalf
- pupil questionnaires to elicit their views.

For pupils who do not attend, the feedback after the meeting is more important in order for the pupil to have a full understanding of what happened during the meeting and the outcomes.

Pupil participation in the statutory assessment process

The Code of Practice (2001) states that 'pupils' views about their needs and difficulties should, wherever possible, be recorded and taken account as part of the statutory assessment process'. When considering ways in which a pupil could contribute towards the statutory assessment process, ensure that the information supplied is written from the pupil's perspective in whatever form. The information could take the form of questionnaires, discussions or materials provided by using pictures, signs, and symbols, audio or video materials. The pupil should be provided with opportunities to consider their needs, strengths, weaknesses, concerns, progress, areas for improvement, what help they need to overcome barriers to learning and who they would like help from. Again, quality feedback after the assessment is essential if the pupil is to understand the support that has been made available and what provision has been made for them at school. As a TA you may be involved in gathering some aspects of this information or assisting the pupil to prepare their own information.

Pupil involvement in teaching and learning

Most of the previous discussion in this chapter has been concerned with pupils with special needs participating in issues related to special provision and statutory frameworks. This section will focus upon ways in which pupils with special needs can be involved in the learning process.

Every teacher knows that truly effective learning and teaching focuses on individual children, their strengths, their needs and the approaches which engage, motivate and inspire them. (DfES 2003)

The starting point for involving pupils in learning and teaching could be the sharing of learning objectives and success criteria. As a TA you may find yourself undertaking this when working with individuals, small groups or the whole class. The aim is to ensure that pupils understand what they need to do, find out what they already know, consider what they would like to know, keep connections clear as the work progresses, and help them to understand the success criteria for individual learners. In this way sharing learning objectives and success criteria focuses more on the learning than the activity and assists the pupils to become more self-evaluative. The impact of sharing the learning objectives should be that the pupils become more focused on the task, they persevere for longer and they focus on the learning intentions rather than their own interests.

Discussions and observations of pupils can also inform how well teaching meets the needs of pupils with SEN. Some useful strategies might include:

- adapting resources/materials to make it relevant and accessible to the pupils
- discussing the learning needs of the pupils with them
- using observation to gain an understanding of the pupils' perspective
- making sure that the pupil knows what equipment will be needed and how to use it
- assisting pupils to organise their thoughts and set out work, e.g. mind-maps
- using interactive methods which ensure participation from all pupils
- ensuring that pupils are aware of how their current work relates to their IEP targets
- valuing mistakes and misconceptions and using them as a way of improving learning
- engaging pupils in peer support and paired work in order to share understanding and discuss their learning
- providing ways in which all pupils can participate in the starting activity and plenary
- providing pupils with strategies to remember information, e.g. writing lists, symbol boards.

Case study

Paul, a Year 3 pupil, finds it difficult to remember the tasks he has to do and their sequence when he gets to school. His TA reminds him to go to his work tray, where he takes out his 'thinking board'. On a vertical strip of Velcro there are several symbols to aid his recall: of a coat, toilet, fridge (to store his lunch), work. As he completes each task, he lifts the symbol off the board and places it in a pocket at the back. On returning to the classroom, he takes his independent work from his tray and completes it. His final task is to remember to give a member of staff his finished card.

(From QCA 2001)

Finally, providing effective feedback is a key element of the learning process and may include oral or written feedback. For more information, refer to Chapter 7 on assessment.

Assisting pupils to become involved in their own learning

Early intervention to develop the skills of decision-making is essential if pupils are to develop the knowledge and skills necessary. They should be involved in making simple choices, expressing preferences or opinions and discussing personal performance from a very early age. For some pupils, early problem-solving may consist of choosing a favourite toy or pushing away an unwanted item; this might develop into expressing simple opinions about likes and dislikes. Some pupils may be able to play little or no part in the decision-making processes, responding rather than initiating, and they may tend to rely upon direction and support from the teacher or other adults. These pupils may remain at this level because of poorly developed skills that are required for decision-making or low adult perceptions and expectations of need or performance.

Ware (2003), in discussions about how it is possible to obtain the views of people with profound and multiple learning difficulties, notes that photos or video could be used to demonstrate what experiences a pupil enjoys and what they do not. Think about whether a photo of a child enjoying a particular activity can be equated with them expressing the view that they want to participate in that activity. Possibly being able to indicate likes and dislikes in ways which are reliably understood by others is an important first step in autonomous decision-making.

Other pupils may be beginning to make decisions about their own needs and learning. They are developing the ability to express likes and dislikes, are learning to see the purpose of an educational activity and beginning to see the point of view of others. The involved pupil is able to make collaborative decisions with the teacher or TA, assesses their own progress and is able to recognise what s/he is good at and their areas of weakness. They are able to recognise personal improvement, work more independently and have a clearer vision about what might be achieved.

In order to support pupils to become involved in their own learning we should assist them to solve problems by using knowledge, memory and thinking skills. TAs should recognise opportunities for pupils to take part in problem-solving activities, whether individually or in groups, which are related to real-life situations.

Pupils need to be helped to break down a problem into small chunks and use thinking skills to plan ways to solve it. Another element is to assist pupils to gain organisational and study skills across all subjects and at each key stage. This includes the ability to direct their attention and follow instructions and sustain interest and attention over longer periods of time.

Pupils need to be taught to manage their personal effects and to organise which equipment will be required for which lesson or where equipment in the classroom is kept. They need to develop an understanding of task completion, take responsibility for completing tasks independently and communicate when they have been completed.